DATE DUE

MAR 1 8 2013

THE ULTIMATE ONLINE CUSTOMER SERVICE GUIDE

How to Connect with Your Customers to
SELL MORE!

MARSHA COLLIER

WILEY

John Wiley & Sons, Inc.

Published by John Wiley & Sons, Inc., Hoboken, New Jersey.
Published simultaneously in Canada.

For general information on our other products and services or for technical support, please contact our Customer Care Department within the United States at (800) 762-2974, outside the United States at (317) 572-3993 or fax (317) 572-4002.

Wiley also publishes its books in a variety of electronic formats. Some content that appears in print may not be available in electronic books. For more information about Wiley products, visit our web site at www.wiley.com.

Library of Congress Cataloging-in-Publication Data:
Collier, Marsha.
The ultimate online customer service guide : how to connect with your customers to sell more! / by Marsha Collier.
p. cm.
Includes index.
ISBN 978-0-470-63770-8 (cloth); ISBN 978-1-118-00763-1 (ebk);
ISBN 978-1-118-00764-8 (ebk); ISBN 978-1-118-00765-5 (ebk)
1. Customer services. 2. Internet marketing. 3. Social media. I. Title.
HF5415.5.C6225 2011
658.8'12—dc22

2010036020

Printed in the United States of America

10 9 8 7 6 5 4 3 2 1

Contents

Introduction

Though I've run a small business for much of my life, I'm a consumer, as well.

It's human nature to desire choice. We want to be able to choose one item over another or one vendor over another, based on a variety of reasons. When we exchange our hard-earned money for an item or a service, we ask for something else in return: to be treated with respect and honesty. We prefer to do business with people "like us," because we want to believe that those we trust to have our best interests at heart. Think about it: Have you ever asked a sales clerk in a clothing store how a particular outfit looked on you? How handsome you looked in that flashy sports car?

I've been writing about eBay for e-commerce vendors for over 12 years, and in that time I've seen thousands of homespun businesses fail in their attempts to become work-from-home moguls. Why? Because many felt—due to the fact that they were selling online—they could omit the personal touch. It made selling so much easier (or so they thought) to never have to actually *deal* with their customers. They thought they could ignore the small niceties that made customers happy to be doing business with them. Time—and a lot of unsuccessful companies—have shown that these assumptions were wrong.

If merchants or service providers put their bottom line before the customer, they will doom their businesses to ultimate failure. They may flourish for a while, maybe even long enough to sell their business to another company and walk away with a healthy profit. But to create a long-term, stable business, you need to have long-term, loyal customers. The best companies grow as a result of positive word of mouth—both in the real world and on the Internet.

Online customer service is an important part of marketing your business. Brilliant, spot-on marketing not only generates revenue for your bottom line; it's also a way to make your customer's life easier. When you give someone quality service, you're a step ahead of your competition.

Most customer service experts fill the books they write and their conference presentations with instructions for growing larger businesses. Though they can charge thousands of dollars for their advice, it's often not completely translatable to a small-staffed enterprise.

I enjoy working with small businesses; they're the bread and butter of our economy. There are a lot more mom-and-pops out there than there are big businesses. As you'll learn in *The Ultimate Online Customer Service Guide*, mom-and-pop businesses can employ more than a hundred people, and without losing their personal attachment to their business. Whether we choose to work in a large or small business environment differs from one person to another, of course; some people are more geared to the detachment inherent in running a big business. However, there are plenty of us who enjoy being part of the daily excitement of running our own companies.

Small businesspeople have the benefit of putting their hearts into what they do, every single day. They truly care about whether their customers enjoy the food, clothing, or the service they provide. It's personal to them; it should be personal to their customers.

I've been working with small and medium businesses for most of my career. I've aided companies that work out of garages, spare rooms, and even barns. I've helped these individuals figure out where they should spend their money to grow, and spoken with them on even the deepest, most personal levels. I've heard from students, newlyweds, career changers, and retirees, and I've found that pretty much everyone has the same goal: They want to make more money. Sadly, however, I've also learned that only a small percentage really wants to work for it.

Those who understand that nothing comes easy, and that the traditional work ethic pays off, become thriving entrepreneurs. Such people become the heart and soul of small business; and it is these small companies that often can reach their customers online much more adeptly than large corporations.

Just how important is small business to our overall economy? As defined by the Small Business Administration (SBA), "small businesses" are those with fewer than 500 employees—a risk-taking, "crazy" group of entrepreneurs who create more than half of the nonfarm, private gross domestic product (GDP) in the United States—yes, more than half. Need more proof as to how important small businesses are to the economic health of our country? These organizations:

- Represent 99.7 percent of all employer firms.
- Employ just over half of all private-sector employees.
- Pay 44 percent of total U.S. private payroll.
- Have generated 64 percent of net new jobs over the past 15 years.

- Hire 40 percent of high-tech workers—like scientists, engineers, and computer programmers.
- Are 52 percent home-based and 2 percent franchises.
- Comprised 97.3 percent of all identified exporters, and produced 30.2 percent of the known export value in 2007.
- Produce 13 times more patents per employee than large patenting firms—patents that are twice as likely as large-firm patents to be among the 1 percent most cited.[1]

An earlier study found that of the 5,369,068 employer firms in the United States, 99.7 percent had fewer than 500 employees, and 78.8 percent had fewer than 10 employees in 1997. More recent data also suggests that very small firms—those with fewer than 10 employees—hire part-time employees at a rate almost twice that of very large firms (1,000 or more employees). If small firms did not hire these part-time employees, they might otherwise be unemployed.

I worked with brick-and-mortar retailers for over a decade, managing advertising and marketing for several super-regional malls (shopping centers with more than 800,000 square feet of leasable area) during their heyday in the 1990s. But just because they were big didn't mean that they always took their customers' needs into consideration.

One Los Angeles center I handled was part of a national chain. The corporate office expected the mall to run the standard advertising program (designed for suburban white neighborhoods) in this center's highly Hispanic market. My proposed idea of running a bilingual campaign, which featured models in

---

[1] U.S. Department of Commerce, Bureau of the Census and International Trade Administration; SBA Advocacy-funded research by Kathryn Kobe and CHI Research, Department of Labor, Bureau of Labor Statistics, 2007.

the ads that reflected members of the community, was seen as heresy—initially. But since sales were falling, they were ready to try my "wacky idea," to respect the predominant customer culture. In retrospect, it seems shocking that my theory was once considered ground-breaking.

Perhaps that's why I felt I *had* to write this book. Much that I see and hear nowadays—including the advice of well-intentioned experts—ignores the human element of business. A good product is paramount, yes, but if there's no personal connection in the way you relate to your customers, you will not succeed. It may take time to fail, but the fall will come. Marketing with the goal of making your customer feel included and part of your community is in your—and your customers'—best interest. It places your business within their trusted circle. Communication is the best way to strengthen your customer's loyalty.

Another of my clients, an e-commerce company, needed me to help them expedite their product photography by automating their storage and shipping. After we implemented changes, the company was running like a Swiss clock. Its profits went from tens of thousands to hundreds of thousands . . . and then I got a call. The company was about to be thrown off of eBay (its largest market at the time). Why, I asked incredulously. Its business model was near-perfect.

Upon arriving at headquarters, I interviewed the people in the customer service department. I learned that their computers were clogged with complaint e-mails, and reps were sending out automated responses without following up with customers. Eventually, the staff began deleting e-mails en masse due to their frustration. I told them they had to make customer service a top priority, that *they* had to make things right. They had to learn how to "take it in the shorts" when they were at fault.

Unfortunately, they didn't take me seriously, and this company ended up spending thousands of dollars on highly billing consultants, to no avail. Customers filed Federal Trade Commission (FTC) complaints, and you can probably guess the outcome. A brilliant business model was ruined due to one organization's lack of concern for its customers. Though it had spent thousands on consultants and fancy marketing tools, without the primary ingredient—respect for the customer—it was doomed.

Perhaps it was the advent of technology that has caused us to stray from the personalization of our businesses. Technology has enabled more people to run successful businesses for a lot less money, a lot of them remotely. Sadly, there's no humanity involved in the kind of technologies that have been sold to businesses.

Since the beginning of civilization, wealth and businesses were built on a simple tenet: Someone sold something to someone else. This is nothing new; it's been this way since biblical times. Whether we're trading, interacting, or selling, we are all customers and vendors in one form or another. Most would argue that this "oldest profession" relies on the exchange of favors for money; but, indeed, the oldest profession is merely a form of entrepreneurship.

At the turn of the century, my great-grandmother supported her three sons by standing on the docks at Ellis Island and buying the long tresses of immigrant women as they came off the ships. (There was an entire community of settlers who made a living from one another. Money for an immigrant in a new country was a huge factor in starting out right, and they all helped each other.) My great-grandmother would then sell the hair to wig makers, whose creations festooned the heads of New York's elite. Though I suppose it was considered a cottage industry back then, my great-grandmother would likely be called an entrepreneur today. Whatever the label, it was a win-win situation for all involved. She worked on trust and reputation. Those weren't easy days for anyone.

Consider *any* job or occupation nowadays. Everything involves selling—taking the risk, developing a business—all for the sake of profit in the end.

But what about employees? Yes, there are ranks of workers who perhaps do not even come in contact with your clients. However, their effort is reflected in your company's bottom line. Your goal for your business is to turn a profit, but you can't do this without customers, and your employees are your conduit to gaining more customers.

Customer service, community, and *trust* aren't just terms for the big guys like the phone company, your credit card provider, or your Internet service provider. It's something we all come to expect from everyone with whom we do business, in one form or another. As a businessperson, you've got to make *customer service* more than a buzzword or phrase. It cannot simply be lip service; rather, it has to be the underlying tenet, the foundation for your business.

In my attempt to become a retail marketing "expert" (though I really don't like that term), I attended seminar after seminar, designed to teach merchants how to "manage" their customers—because customers are the lifeblood of commerce. I sat in big rooms with groups of small businesspeople like myself. I listened to the speakers (because I was told they were experts) and absorbed as much as I could. I admit that I sat there like the rest of the audience, nodding my head in agreement with the presenters, even when I really wasn't sure what they were talking about. In fact, we looked like a sea of bobble-head dolls. Looking back, I wonder if anyone else besides me felt that only a small percentage of what the speakers were saying really applied to my business situation.

When we attend such conferences, we often get wrapped up in the plethora of acronyms: VRM, CRM, ACES . . . (they *do* go on). We learn; we listen to the experts; we nod our heads in agreement and vow to follow the latest and greatest customer acquisition and satisfaction methods.

A note here on the use of acronyms: I will not use acronyms in this book; instead, I will use the actual words, and define the more popular ones. Too many of us often fall into the habit of using this kind of techno-jargon because the terms fly off the tongue so easily, making our conversation seem so much more efficient. But using acronyms can make communication less meaningful and more unintelligible for those who do not use or hear them regularly. It's too easy to forget, for example, that the "C" in CRM stands for *customer*. Our customers are not just a "C," and we must never lose sight of that.

We read blogs and books, attend these conferences, and listen to the experts, all the while trying to make a complicated science out of a basic human need: the desire to be treated with respect. We are all clients, customers, patients, consumers, shoppers; we all exchange money for services and merchandise. As consumers with choices, we can go anywhere we want to spend our money. The one thing we all have in common is that we are human beings. As human beings, we hope to maintain a little dignity in our everyday lives—including when we make buying decisions. We hope that manufacturers and providers will have a little respect for us and our family.

Respect for your customer—and the hard-earned money they pay for your service or merchandise—is the key to giving superior customer service.

Our society used to care whether we got value for our dollars. But lately, we just seem to be looking for the cheapest, quickest, easiest way to acquire products and services. In this process, we don't always respect the seller or supplier, do we? Yet when we get lousy, disrespectful treatment, it makes us angry and annoyed.

You might say that, in many instances, human respect—both toward and from our vendors—has diminished significantly in recent years. We need to turn this around and begin to provide a good customer experience for *all* customers, without charging ridiculously high prices.

Where do *you* go to complain when you feel that you've been wronged by a business? What happens when something goes awry? Who do you turn to? That's when we pay the high cost for our low expectations.

We have lots of new tools on the Internet—specifically, within social media—that are meant to help us engage and interact with our customers. And, again, there are a lot of experts out there who are making fortunes showing us how to use these tools. Blogs and Web sites like Facebook and Twitter are the shiny new things. In fact, many claim to be the panacea that will make all our customer service woes disappear—*and* bring millions to our doors.

I've always put my e-mail address in the introduction of all my books, and tried to make myself accessible to anyone who writes to me. Considering the number of books I've sold over the past few years—well, you can just imagine how many people have contacted me. And though it's taken a lot of my time, I want to hear stories of businesses that thrive, and I enjoy seeing people overcome their problems on the way to success—because I really do care when someone reads my words and acts on them. I want to know what worked—and what didn't—in order to better serve my future readers.

I also get e-mails every day from readers of my Google profile, blog, or the feedback on my Web site, www.coolebaytools .com. While there is a disclaimer on my Web site that states that I can't always respond to every e-mail I get, I guarantee that I read them all—and I *do*. I receive questions that run the gamut from basic to advanced, and it can be overwhelming at times. I often find myself resisting the urge to say, "You can find that information on page 126 of *Title XYZ*." I answer as often as I can, and try to be helpful—because I know that in order to keep an online community alive, both my supporters and I must remain active within it.

Social media can do all that and more. In *The Ultimate Online Customer Service Guide*, I will use everyday examples to show you how businesses are doing it right, as well as discuss those that are doing it wrong.

You can build a *community* with your customers. That's another term we hear a lot of these days. But community has always been the backbone of trust. Great-grandma had her community of immigrants, who supported each other and kept in contact. In the early days of our country, communities were formed to help people develop a feeling of worth. In the 1950s, they met at Floyd's barber shop and shared their daily news and gossip. In the 1990s, our communities took the form of malls, where everyone shopped, met for lunch, and attended events.

We have always embraced communities for introducing us to people with whom we have things in common. Nowadays, these communities are centered not only around schools and churches, sports and hobbies, but we can also find them on the Internet.

Community has likewise become part of corporate culture—and when it's done right, it becomes the basis of how we do business. Remember: Your customer is a human being. *You* are a human being. We thrive on respect and being part of a community. I hate to throw out a cliché like, "Do unto others . . ." but it's appropriate here.

Years ago, when someone had a lousy experience with a business, he or she passed on those negative feelings to perhaps 20 of his or her friends. Today, via the use of social media, a single one of your customers can broadcast a message to a million of his or her "closest acquaintances."

Whether you have a retail location or a business practice—whether you even ever physically interact with your customer—you *can* ensure that you have happy customers. Your customers should always walk away from an interaction with you with a feeling of wonder—the feeling of "wow."

Joseph Jaffe, a noted thought leader on new marketing and president of crayon, described as "a strategic consultancy that helps its clients achieve positive change and impact by joining the conversation," has always been a fan of following the customer's humanity. I met him several years ago and have continually enjoyed his vocal, honest perspectives. In his recent "Customer Service Manifesto" he echoed the philosophy of this book when he wrote, "Loving thy neighbor has always made good sense. Having a customer who loves you back in return makes for good business sense."

So hang in there with me and read on. I promise, no jargon or absolutes; just real-world examples and truths—that you *already* know. All you have to do is follow your instincts, while you pick up some additional tips on how to connect with your customers online.

1

The Art of Customer Service

Why, you might wonder, would one use the word *art* to describe a business practice like customer service? After all, most of business is pretty cut-and-dried, whereas we often think of those who have artistic talent as touchy-feely types—as being less logical and more right-brained than successful, professional types—right?

Not necessarily. American neurobiologist Roger W. Sperry first introduced the concept of right-brain and left-brain thinking in the late 1960s. Sperry's research showed that the human brain has two very different ways of thinking. The right brain is visually oriented and processes information in an intuitive and synchronized way, while the left brain processes information in an analytical and sequential way. In 1981, Sperry won the Nobel Prize in Medicine for his work in split-brain research.

We all have two ways of processing information, and as vendors of products or services, we need to appeal to both. Overly creative right-brainers tend to get a bad rap these days. They are thought of as dreamers, visionaries, or idealistic enthusiasts; rarely as sharp, savvy businesspeople. This doesn't make a lot of sense when you look at it through the lens of today's forward-thinking CEOs—many of whom, by the way, say that the way they make decisions is based largely on intuition, because all the data they need is not always available and they must be able to react quickly to the market.

Take Kip Tindell, CEO of the Container Store. He was quoted in the *New York Times* (March 13, 2010) as saying, "We just beg and plead and try to get employees to believe that intuition does have a place in the workforce. After all, intuition is only the sum total of your life experience. So why would you want to leave it at home when you come to work in the morning?"

Columbia University Business School offers a course for executives that teaches them to make better use of their intuition. The course is based on William Duggan's publicly acclaimed series of books, *Strategic Intuition: The Key to Innovation*, and introduces breakthrough ideas, methods, and tools for generating creative ideas that are also strategic.

"The only real valuable thing is intuition."

—ALBERT EINSTEIN

If you look, you'll find plenty of examples of leaders using their intuition. Leading by intuition does not mean making uninformed or sporadic decisions. To the contrary: You as a leader need to make sure that your instincts are fully supported by information from your customer and employees. This means that by being involved in online outreach you receive constant feeds from your target market and your employees. By tapping into what your customers need and want, and how those demands are or are not being met by those who regularly interact with them, you will be in a stronger position to use your intuition more effectively.

Therein lies the opportunity for your customer service engagement. With your online presence, you are in the position to regularly interact with customers. You have the opportunity to see what works and what doesn't. Knowledge gleaned from outside your inner sanctum will enable you to address key questions, such as whether your product or service offering is right for the market and up to date with current trends. This helps you motivate employees to deliver the level of service required and to identify what, if any, are opportunities for your company's growth.

Interestingly, that has been the main focus of former Forrester analyst, Dr. Natalie Petouhoff (@DrNatalie on Twitter). At Forrester, she covered not only customer service and customer relationship management (CRM), but by observing the new juncture of social media and those disciplines, she wrote the world's first social media return on investment (ROI) model.

Natalie, now the chief social media and digital communication strategist at Weber Shandwick, is one of the truly brilliant folks in her field; her work is legendary at businesses whose budgets we can only imagine.

Her groundbreaking ideas in this arena can help to center our thoughts on exactly how this is all going to work for our own businesses. When I asked Dr. Natalie about my theory about customer service becoming the new marketing, and about how small business has an innate advantage today, here's what she shared with me:

People asked me why I went from addressing customer service and its professionals to a public relations and marketing firm. What I found was that companies are fracturing their brands. This started to happen even before social media.

PR and marketing departments were crafting amazing brand promises. But because the way those departments have been organized, they don't interact with customers after the brand promise has been delivered. So who does have to deliver on the brand promise? Customer service. And because customer service has been largely trapped into the category of a cost center, it rarely is able, during those customer interactions, to deliver on the brand promise, or even have enough respect within the organization to have others accept the idea [that] they have to change products or services to better meet customers' wants and needs.

This dynamic—the lack of interdepartmental interaction—has been happening since companies left the mom-and-pop model. Along comes social media, and what are consumers using it for? Among the many uses—to keep in touch with friends and family, find a lost love, shop—they are realizing they can broadcast to millions their disdain about how companies are *not* meeting their brand promise.

As a management consultant back in the days of the top management consulting companies, (the "Big 6," including Accenture, Price Waterhouse, Coopers & Lybrand, Ersnt & Young), as a PricewaterhouseCoopers consultant, we were taught that more than anything, managing customer expectations was the key to success. And that lesson learned can be applied here today in business.

That is the reason I joined a PR and marketing firm. I wanted to help companies manage their customers' expectations. After many years in the corporate world, I realized the chasm in corporations needed to be healed. That chasm? Interdepartmental disconnect and dysfunction. If I were to really help the business world make this huge change, I myself had to be the change. I had to partner with professionals in departments that I might not have ordinarily interfaced with. So I joined a PR and marketing firm.

I saw that PR and marketing had mastery over delivering a brand's promise. And that their worth was based on the ability to help customers become aware, and to consider purchasing products and services from their company. Once sales "closed the deal," customer service's role was to help, answer questions, and solve problems.

The disconnect was that PR and marketing professionals were not always delivering a brand promise that customer service could consistently provide. And, note, none of this was the fault of PR, marketers, or customer service. It was an artifact of how companies organize themselves into groups of specialties; and rarely do they have leadership that has the intuition that continuing to interact as disparate silos not only is *not* in the best interest of any of those departments, [but that] it will actually be the downfall of companies, which will go out of business if they don't "get it." Of the companies that do sense some of this, many of them may not know how to break down the silos in the politically charged situations they work in. And even in the best situations, they certainly would not be compensated for interdepartmental collaboration.

What social media is doing for companies is essentially this: It is a source of real-time feedback. That feedback is filled with information, if you are listening, that can be used to change your products and service to meet your customers' needs. Imagine how much easier it would be to market and sell a product [that] your customers said they wanted. Imagine if you are listening to your customers and you are using [what they're saying] for product innovation. Imagine if your competitor is not. Imagine the market advantage you'd have. And imagine if you used customer service as your differentiator. Why would your customers go anywhere else?

While companies are either blindly hobbling along, doing things the way they always have done, or perhaps noticing something probably needs to change, the customer has taken things into [his or her] own hands.

Customers have realized that posting on Twitter, Facebook, blogs, and other places got the attention of millions. Customers are avoiding calling the call center, and instead are going to social media to announce their disappointment and disdain. The power of social media has put the power into the hands of the customer.

If companies had gotten ahead of these issues and made the changes they needed to make so that the PR and marketing brand messaging could be delivered by the products and service, as well as by customer service, many companies would not be doing the social media scramble. But they didn't.

Some of these ideas are not really new, but the intuitive leader will respond to issues arising from this information more quickly and effectively, and ensure the structures are in place to achieve it.

PR has now become customer service. Customer service in now PR. The question you have to ask yourself is, "How are you going to be managing the expectations of your customers, and how will all your departments deliver on your brand's promise?" No customers, no business. Period.

Natalie's words on silos (departments or people who do not share information) are the last you will read in this book. As a small businessperson, you have too much on the line. Rather than forming silos in your organization, you can encourage collaboration with your employees and develop engagement with your customers. You can work as a *team*.

My experience tells me that customer service is not only an art, but a "soft science." By *soft science*, I don't mean that there are no concrete numbers to run the business. There are specific rules that must be followed and will always work for all situations. But there are also numerous ways to perform quality customer service, depending on the customer and the situation.

Of course, those who manage customer service will say it's easier to manage people working in customer service when there are clear rules that govern how they treat customers. But it's following those rules to a tee (even when you and your employees know doing so doesn't make sense) is what incenses customers and will probably lead to employee attrition at your company.

Instead, consider this: Art is a means to an end; it is the deployment of words and actions to accomplish a task. Art can facilitate constructive interactions. To have mastery at one's "art" requires practice and a certain amount of reverence. If may seem strange to think that something as basic as customer service has to become an art—or at the very least, a soft science with a range of approaches—but I think what you will find in this book is that if you can learn and apply this idea, not only will you be happier in your work, so will your employees. Your customers will also return and stay loyal. The point is, working from this starting point allows us to better understand the ongoing process of forming connections with our customers.

Developing Your Customer Service Intuition Skills

The art of serving customers begins with creating real relationships with real people in the real world. For years, we didn't connect the brick-and-mortar aspect of business to the online world. It's important to make sure that no matter where we are dealing with customers—in a store, on the phone, or on a Web site—there are some basic tenets to keep in mind.

To perform quality customer service, you need to respect, trust, and be committed to the people you are dealing with. This is a core tenet. A culture and a lifestyle of treating others with the same respect you wish to be treated is key to reducing attrition and strengthening customer loyalty.

What's funny is that this is all you need to know. It's customer service, in a nutshell. It's everything your parents (and, hopefully, teachers) tried to instill in you as a child. We were brought up thinking that respect for others was the key to a good life. So exactly when did this change? Just because we're living in the dollars-and-cents business world?

At what point did we begin to think that it was acceptable to ask employees to work more hours than we pay them for? Or to make cuts in staff when it comes to customer service, when it's the task that is the most customer-oriented? When did we begin to think it was "good enough" to *not* treat others as we would like to be treated ourselves—even worse, to *not* treat customers the way *they* want to be treated?

When researching what the "big brains" (you know, the experts with all the answers) thought about customer service, I scoured scores of high-level books written by high-powered specialists. Some of them I bookmarked, and a very few are marked throughout with highlighter. These books are mostly about promoting loyalty in the old-school style. The others are treatises, full of data and charts; and most claimed to have some supernatural key to success. When it comes to customer service, working with people is not cut-and-dried. People are not numbers.

So why is this "magic bullet" so difficult for so many to recognize?

Top business experts spend a lot of time putting things into categories: customers, employees, situations. There are tons of charts, along with a multitude of acronyms, which reduce simple human needs to statistics and alphabet soup. But we're not statistics or letters; we're people.

The bottom line is, there was little "humanity" in the bulk of the books I read. No art. In them, customers were reduced to statistics—not for the purpose of understanding them, but to teach how to "get them." People have feelings. They have expectations. They have wants, needs, and desires, and we as business owners need to make sure that our products, services, and messages can deliver on all that.

The quote here is something we should all keep in mind, as it applies to each and every one of us in business:

> "The only value a company has is the value that comes from customers: the ones they have now and the ones in the future."
>
> —Don Peppers and Martha Rogers, PhD

Do Lessons Learned from Large Companies Apply to Your Business?

There's also a huge disconnect between small and large business. Small businesses have the advantage of being closer to their customers and employees. They've retained more of the mom-and-pop feel to their businesses. The acronyms that the experts like to use are only vaguely part of the small-business dialogue. We know the words, and recognize that a customer is a person, not a "C." Small business interacts with customers every day.

A lot of these graduate-schooled, powerful experts love the graphs and charts, whereas small business has very little time for these. We're in the trenches, and although we may produce a graph every now and then, we certainly don't run our companies based on them.

When the Light Came On

All data has its place with all of us—including top-level planners—and though the statistics portion of business is important, short text in an article or blog often delivers more information. If there is something to be learned, I want to learn it as quickly as possible.

I've heard that, last year, top companies spent over $450 billion in new customer acquisition, yet spent only $50 billion on customer service. Whether this figure is fact or apocryphal, it seems upside down to me. If these organizations were actually putting their money where their mouths are, customer service and promoting customer loyalty would be the *top* figure. I guess if you continue to burn out your customers with poor-quality service, you'd better be prepared to pony up some new consumers to support the bottom line.

At the point in my career when I lived and breathed the stats, I met a man named Peter Glen. I was building the fashion section for a soon-to-be prominent newspaper, and Peter was brought in to cement our connections with top retailers. He was a fascinating and provocative man; you either loved or hated him. He showed up for conferences well dressed, with a crazy bow tie and red socks or some other accessory to make a visual point that thinking and acting outside the box was his norm.

Peter had established a reputation as the top retail consultant in the country. He was the original "push-the-envelope" kind of guy. He authored several books, including *It's Not My Department: How America Can Return to Excellence—Giving and Receiving Quality Service* (Berkley Trade, 1992). Although it's been almost 20 years since its publication, Peter's words are still valid today.

Peter was such a force in motivating retailers to produce fine service that when he died in 2001, the National Retail Federation created the Peter Glen Retailer of the Year award, given to the retailer that best exemplifies Glen's standards of retail excellence: innovation, service and intelligence. He left a legacy of quality.

In an interview in early 2001, Peter applied his visionary thinking to the future of online retail commerce:

> E-commerce would have you believe the merchandise doesn't matter—that it's all in the distribution business. That's changing fast. Merchants are moving onto the Internet, [and] a merchant at the helm is still the competitive difference between one Web site and another—[between] good merchants and bad, those who get it and those who don't.

The merchants who "get it" are the ones who display exemplary customer service.

How interesting to read these thoughts from a time when very few people knew where e-commerce was going. Peter would consult with shopping centers and retailers, using the original "secret shopper" program as part of his research; and when he reported in, the results were rarely up to his standards. Relating to, respecting, and dignifying customer service were his top goals. I remember him asking the crowd of well-dressed, big-brained retail executives for whom he consulted, "Who has seen *E.T.* (referring to Steven Spielberg's now-classic film, *E.T. the Extra Terrestrial*)?"

There were mutterings from participants all around about how their kids had seen it, and that it was certainly a kid's movie; but only a couple of people raised their hands. To this, Peter responded with another question, "How can you possibly relate to your customer if you're not understanding pop culture? This is what they are watching, and it affects their thinking and what they want."

Peter was indeed a futurist. He made me realize that there's a line between those who "get it" and those who don't. And you need to "get" the art of customer service, too.

If a cultural shift is taking place, you should be aware of it. Anytime a change in customers' lives occurs, it is an opportunity to provide better service, but only if you understand exactly what is flipping their switch at the moment.

That's the art: understanding your customers, and knowing what they like. Peter often said, "Retailing is theater." He felt that engaging the customer was best done with bells and whistles and honesty—and art.

Respecting your customer by delivering the finest service is the main cog in the wheel of customer loyalty. In this world of infinitely fast electronic communication, a loyal customer is your best secret weapon.

What Is the Business Value of Customer Service?

In 2007, a report from Walker Information, Inc. (a worldwide leader in customer loyalty management), titled "The Walker Loyalty Report for Online Retail," exposed some telling figures about the companies that obtain the top customer loyalty ratings. The report averaged three years' worth of revenue data and found, interestingly, that the average operating income of those companies they deemed as "Loyalty Leaders" grew 682 percent higher than those that scored low in customer loyalty. Their annual revenue growth was 146 percent. The study also found that among satisfied customers in a range of industries, only about 50 percent were loyal. These numbers send a clear message to anyone who cares about their bottom line.

There are—at a minimum—five things you must absolutely do to keep customers in a "good mood." This good mood may garner sales and bring them back to your Web site to shop over and over—that is, if you play your cards right.

1. *Welcome the customer.* This is more than just having a lovely homepage. Let the customers know—at first contact—how important they are to you and your business.
2. *Offer help at each step of the way.* Not everyone is as Web savvy as you are (or your employees); make sure your site is easy to navigate and has a help button at every turn. Make your forms simple.
3. *Give customers space.* Don't have bouncing "Can I help you?" bubbles traveling back and forth across the page. Did you know that these make some people nervous? Perhaps that's why they exit many online stores.
4. *Offer customers more than just merchandise for sale.* People crave information about what they buy.
5. *Thank them.* A thank-you is not an offer for a small, free item tied to a subscription to a newsletter. A thank-you is your heartfelt way of letting customers know you're truly happy for their patronage. Offer a coupon for future use, or a discount on their next order—anything to make 'em smile!

Remember that "online" means connecting on the Web. Like a spider web, there are myriad platforms from which to connect, join, and relate to your customers.

A Word from a "Soft Scientist"

While I was writing this book, I spoke to a lot of people who study customer service for a living. I like to think of them as the "big brains." I respect them, and so I looked to them to find alternate definitions of the *art of customer service.*

I called on Michael Krigsman, chief executive officer of Asuret, Inc., a consulting company that studies and prevents failed information technology (IT) projects. He's also a prominent blogger and expert on topics related to social media, customer relationship management, and leadership.

That said, Michael knows his stuff on some very high levels. When we spoke about the future of customer service online, he spoke some pretty solid words to me.

> Customers have become an important "power bloc" in their own right. Gone are the days when we can control the customer relationship, filtering our message and expecting customers to sit back and smile. Today, social tools such as Twitter and Facebook mean that customers can form ad hoc, self-aware interest groups with rapid, even viral, speed.
>
> Today's customers are sophisticated and will take to the online streets in a heartbeat. If they love your product and service, they'll tell their friends. If the call center kept them on hold for an hour, only to be followed by a rude interaction with an inexperienced agent, your customers will shout that from the rooftops.
>
> Wise companies today engage and collaborate with customers to achieve mutual and beneficial value. Invite customers to share their feedback with you, and ask their advice on how to improve. You don't have to accept every bit of advice they offer, but give customers an opportunity to talk. Listen closely to see how you can align customer interests with your goals.
>
> Profitable relationships result when both buyer and seller realize mutual value. In today's world, that's a mantra for communication, engagement, and collaboration.

Michael's words ring true, and align with the message of this book. Humanity and engagement *must* be part of your customer service strategy.

What Online Customer Service Means to You

Why bother with online customer service? After all, don't you believe that you do a good enough job at your business or with your phone response? You know that the world is changing and that people are way too busy to sit through lengthy phone calls. Many no longer want to spend their time on the phone or engaged in chats with canned robots.

In the old days, families used to sit together in the evenings and watch TV. This isn't the case anymore. We live in the electronic age. Everyone is online now and life runs at a much faster pace.

Your customers need to be assured they can reach your business anywhere, anytime, and almost immediately. Quality customer service means providing a convenient place where your company can be contacted whenever your customer has a problem. Online—and specifically through social media—is the best way to enable that reach.

Small businesses don't always have the time or staff to spend on the phone. Your office is often stretched with work as it is. Unfortunately, your customers won't understand; as far as they're concerned, your number one priority is to meet their needs.

Online customer service is useful to you and to your customers, because it (hopefully) allows them to get their messages to you and receive responses back in—at most—24 hours. They can complete what they need to accomplish and move on to the more important things—like living their lives.

If they call your company on the phone and are put on hold for long periods of time, they will grow frustrated and angry— and, therefore, be much more difficult to work with. Getting an answer back from you quickly is important both to them and to your reputation.

It's a well-known fact that the better the customer service experience, the more customers will buy from you—and the more loyal they will be. So having a solid online customer service presence helps you in several ways. It gives your customers some real-world benefits, because it's:

1. *Useful.* By connecting with your company online, customers have an "ear" for describing their dealings with your products, or you and your employees.
2. *Easy.* They can log on to your Web site or blog or connect with you through a social media venue and reach you quickly.
3. *Enjoyable.* By connecting directly, they feel that they've accomplished something; they know their words were heard.

Never lose sight of your customer culture and the value of the relationships the Internet offers your company. And because online customer service has its roots in the real world, consider real-world examples of customer service. Then we can translate what we do face to face into the magic we perform online.

2

Quality Real-World, Small-Business Customer Service

Every day that passes bring us into a new era. As much as we feel comfortable, and often don't notice change, change is inevitable and we adapt. Our way of living transforms from generation to generation. My grandfather used to tell me stories of when the gas-lights in New York City were converted to electric lights—what a miracle it was! Electricity came to the streets of New York around 1900; look how far we've come in a century. (My grandfather would probably seize at the sight of a magical marvel like the iPhone.)

Regardless how much change occurs, however, we still remain human beings, with the same basic needs and wants. A shop-keeper at the turn of the century grew his customer base in the same way we do today: selection, price, and service. But service is what keeps people coming back.

The following is a short list of companies that reads like a who's who of retail. What's remarkable is that most of these companies were founded long before the streets of Manhattan and other cities were fully electrified.

Tiffany & Co., 1837
American Express, 1850
Marshall Field's, 1852
Orvis, 1856
Macy's, 1858
Bloomingdale's, 1860
Spiegel, 1865
Barnes & Noble, 1873
Sears, 1886
Saks Fifth Avenue, 1898
Nordstrom, 1901
JC Penney, 1902
Stein Mart, 1902
Neiman Marcus, 1907
Boscov's, 1911
L.L. Bean, 1912

There's a common thread running throughout these companies, from their founding day until today: the desire to serve their customers well. That's what longevity in business is all about. There will always be financial ups and downs, which are solved by good management (that's where the MBAs come in), but without a core desire to be of service—a *core culture*, as we say today—there is no longevity in business.

What's even more amazing? All these companies have an online presence today; they're communicating with their customers in a new medium. That's "real-world" retail success.

The "real" world is different for us, as well. In our day-to-day lives we communicate with our friends and family; but we also converse online. The way we speak to the different people we see during our days can vary wildly. It feels strange that we need to differentiate between what we do in the real world and what we do online. But we must. How we handle our relationships and communications face to face is rarely the same as how we do so online. Hopefully, in a personal situation, we can be ourselves. In the business world? It's not always that easy.

Believe it or not, there does not need to be much of a difference between how we connect with our friends and how we connect with our customers. However, most people put on their "business face" on when they appear online in a professional capacity, necessitating a bit more formal tone. We need to learn to translate our real-world personal values into the virtual world. But before we go there, let's consider some examples of unique real-world settings.

To see which big-time retailers are doing the best job with customer service in the real world, we can look to the 2009 National Retail Federation (NRF) Customers' Choice awards (sponsored by American Express), which honor retailers across all channels. (Chapter 9, "Platforms to Enhance the Experience," gives you the background on these awards and a little history). It's significant to note that although all these stores have an online presence, only two were founded on the Web.

It will come as no surprise to anyone who's ever shopped there that L.L. Bean was ranked number one in customer service. Number two, Overstock.com, *is* a surprise, considering it is a discount retailer. At number three was Zappos.com; number four, Amazon.com; and number five, QVC. Others in the top 10 were Coldwater Creek, Lands' End, JC Penney, and HSN (Home Shopping Network); tied for 10th were Nordstrom and Kohl's.

Another surprise on the list was that Nordstrom had slipped to number 10—a significant piece of information, considering that the retailer, started as a family-run business, was built on customer service. Founder John Nordstrom admitted that he didn't know whether the size of the first pair of shoes that he sold, in 1901, was correct, but the customer liked them and bought them, thus instituting the Nordstrom theme, "Do whatever it takes to satisfy the customer." Although customer service is the company's byword, some feel its personal touch may be losing to the quest for bottom-line profits.

Check out these face-to-face business examples in the next section and see if they don't lead you to some ideas of how *you* can begin to improve your connections with your particular brand of customer.

A Little Research

Research is the key to success for any level of enterprise. Whether you are a one-person service business, a fully staffed retail location, or a major corporation, taking the time to do your homework pays off. Finding out what your customers (or prospective customers) need and want from your business will quickly give you a leg up on your competition. The alternative is the school of hard knocks, which can be very expensive. Luckily you have this book, and I've done some of the leg work for you.

In today's world we are barraged with companies that receive awards for being the best this and the best that. If you think you can use the same techniques that these large corporations do, you may be missing the point. Small business can rarely mimic a major commercial enterprise's efforts. But by observing which companies are doing things right, you can gain solid insights.

Certainly anyone who has bought a car has heard of the J.D. Power and Associates Awards. A couple of weeks after you buy a new car, the firm sends you a survey to fill out. On this survey, you are asked to rate how well you think your transaction was handled by the dealer. (Ever wonder why new-car dealers are so darned nice to you when you pick up your car?) This same type of pleasant opening tactic is often proffered when you are buying an insurance policy, selecting an airline, or choosing a wireless provider.

J.D. Power also performs hundreds of thousands of surveys each year to determine which companies are the best in each category. Its research compiles data on a range of industries, including airlines, finance, telecoms, healthcare, and automakers. Let's delve a little deeper into what makes up the awards.

J.D. Power and Associates is a marketing research company that has craftily turned the performance of customer satisfaction surveys into a very lucrative business. By publicizing the results of its surveys, it has built a very strong reputation in the customer satisfaction field.

Rather than use stars in its ratings, J.D. Power uses "Power Circles"; five circles is best, four is less good, and so on. These circles represent how products or companies compare against similar ones in their markets. The best-in-class earn five circles and win the coveted award. Sounds pretty fair.

J.D. Power's profits come from corporations that seek access to data from these independently produced, self-funded surveys. Note, however, that not all the data is available to the public. Only top-level highlights of the firm's syndicated studies are available on its Web site, JDPower.com. Should you see a company being advertised as an award winner, know that only the highest ranked are permitted to promote the award; and the right to display the award icon requires a paid license.

By going to JDPower.com, you can view many major companies in fields such as your own; and by doing a little research you can learn exactly what they are doing (right or wrong) to earn their current rating.

Big companies with lots of layers are often slow to change, so those that invest in this research are clearly taking a step forward to improve with the times. Others, even with data in hand, are so set in their old ways that moving forward becomes almost a physical impossibility. J.D. Power recently started marketing Web Intelligence, a social media market research product, to show clients the who, when, and where of online influencers.

There are plenty of ways that you can find information on your company without resorting to the old-school studies (or paying high dollar amounts to a consultant). It's all about observing and engaging when you can, and using online media tools to position your business to best serve your customer. I'll talk further in Chapter 9 about online reputation management platforms.

The New Retail: It's All about Entertainment

It's not enough these days to have an enormous and broad variety of merchandise; visiting a store also needs to be entertaining for the mind and exciting to the eye. Whether stores engage their customers with unique merchandise through visual merchandising or entertain with hands-on product demonstrations, they build interest from the moment the customer enters. (Perhaps even an offer of a cool drink when the customer enters the store?) Engagement comes in many forms.

These days, Apple stores do a stellar job of making retailing almost theater. Going into an Apple store is stimulating on many levels. It's cleanly laid out and full of engaging displays, sights, sounds, and colors. The employees wear different color shirts to define their jobs, making everything and everyone easy to figure out. The shirts originally defined positions with specific slogans:

- *Specialist*: "I can talk about this stuff for hours."
- *Concierge*: "I know people."
- *Creative*: "No pain, all gain."
- *Genius*: "Not all heroes wear capes."
- *Manager*: "My place. Your place."
- *Back-of-house*: "Some artists use brushes. I prefer boxes."

Innovate is what Apple has done. When it came to store planning, Apple controlled everything, and left nothing to chance. The design from the get-go was exacting: to reflect the entertainment quotient of the store. The company used award-winning architecture; large-front windows with interactive displays (even the window glass is specified to be a special, low-iron, water-white glass that has a higher visible transmittance); merchandise grouped in solution zones for hands-on use; theaters, or circular Studio Bars, for demonstrations and instruction; a Genius Bar, for tech support; a children's area; events; and more.

Ron Johnson, Apple's senior vice president of retail commented at a 2006 conference about the design of the company store: "I imagined it as a store for everyone, a place that would be welcoming to all ages, and where people could feel they truly belonged."

The detail is not just in the store; employees are imbued with the Apple "Steps of Service":

A: *Approach* customers with a personalized warm welcome.
P: *Probe* politely, to understand all the customer's needs.
P: *Present* a solution for the customer to take home today.
L: *Listen* for and resolve any issues or concerns.
E: *End* with a fond farewell and an invitation to return.

sart68 At the **Apple Store**. Drooling.
2 minutes ago from Twitterrific

kitfisto Twittando da **apple store**! Acabei de passar na game
stop e comprar o rock band bundle e super mario bros pra wii!
4 minutes ago from Twitterrific

pitpov Props to the willow bend **apple store** for fixin my iPhone.
The glass started to pop out!
5 minutes ago from Tweetie

religionbites At the **Apple Store** with my Dad. We're bringing my
parents over to the dark side. Well, we do have cookies.
6 minutes ago from Echofon

JJincproduction MALL! AGAIN! **APPLE STORE!** AGAIN! WAZ
UP! AGAIN! :D
6 minutes ago from web

kdeeds Enjoyed first **Apple Store** experience. Going to get IPod
Touch. Just got last December paycheck today.
7 minutes ago from web

Figure 2.1   Five minutes' worth of Twitter comments.

What makes the Apple store so desirable? It's today. It's engaging; it's entertaining; and employees genuinely are fans of the products. Figure 2.1 presents a shot of a Twitter search for Apple Store. People *love* the place.

According to posts I've read on the Internet, if you're not an Apple enthusiast, you may not be exactly wowed by the store's customer service. But Apple knows its customers and caters to them in every way possible.

If you have a retail location, have you given the strict eye to detail that Apple has? Even without a large budget, you can accomplish your own Apple magic:

1. Reexamine the lighting in your location, and brighten up your display areas.

2. Categorize your products in a flow that will be pleasing to the eye.
3. Arrange sell-up merchandise closely together.
4. Consider hosting educational events for your customers (and, perhaps, their families).
5. Create your own "steps of service" and post it in your prep area, to inspire your employees.

Engaging Your Clients and Patients

Creating a friendly, welcoming environment goes a long way toward building customer satisfaction. When someone walks into your offices, are they piqued or pleased? Lawyers, doctors—you're the ones I'm talking to here.

When was the last time you redecorated your office? Fifteen years ago? Everyone can follow the example of a retail store that creates an inviting environment. Your waiting room is the first impression you give your clients or patients—your customers. Your private office may be cluttered, but public areas should invoke your professionalism. Is there anything more annoying than sitting in a waiting room with old magazines, bland walls, and scuffed furniture? You need to build confidence from the moment people walk through your door. Straddling the line between professional and comfortable surroundings is an art.

After a recent customer service chat on Twitter, many people drew attention to the fact that the worst customer service they receive is from their doctors. One participant commented, "I would say the doctor's office cared more about verifying insurance than taking an emergency patient." Is this the first impression your patients get from your reception desk?

Upon graduation from medical school, all doctors are required to take an oath. The traditional Hippocratic oath has been replaced by newer versions, and a more popular Oath of

Geneva. Whichever oath a doctor takes, by doing so, he or she is committing to serve his or her patients. But as in any profession, some do it right and others don't.

I contacted two well-respected doctors in different parts of the country to find out what, aside from their medical acumen, made their patients so happy with them. How did they deliver exceptional customer service in their daily practices?

The information from these two doctors can be applied to any business/customer relationship. There are many in the medical profession who do have heart (in addition to experience, talent, and expertise), and respect their customers (patients).

The first of the two, a Los Angeles practicing endocrinologist, is Dr. Joshua Rokaw, past chairman of medicine at a local hospital. He said he felt his office staff did a good job of servicing patients. The office's online reviews were good, so what are they doing right? To start with, they follow a credo as to how they relate to their patients.

- They make sure to honor the oath to protect and respect human life.
- When talking to a patient, Dr. Rokaw always sits down and speaks to patients at eye level. He makes a point to never, in reality or figuratively, talk down to a person.
- Understanding that patients are nervous, Dr. Rokaw knows he must anticipate their fears, and sympathize. Patients are a lot more open with you when they think you "get it."
- After completing lists of questions, Dr. Rokaw's staff always asks what else is on the patient's mind.
- It's important to always discreetly ask about a patient's family life. The reason? The human touch. "Otherwise," says Dr. Rokaw, "doctoring can become a job. It could be done by a computer."

The second doctor I spoke to is a pediatric cardiologist from Dallas, Texas, Dr. Andrew Fryer. Certainly, someone who deals with stressed-out people on a daily basis would have to go the extra mile for his patients (customers); but even more, he deals with sick, and often scared, children.

Dr. Fryer brings humanity to a clinical setting. He finds that the patient compliance rate goes up when he forms trusting relationships with his patients and their families. To build such relationships he follows his own set of rules:

- When talking to a patient, he listens and makes eye contact. He doesn't stare at a piece of paper.
- He jokes around with children, using self-deprecating humor to help put them at ease.
- His staff routinely pays a lot of attention to the children, as well as their parents.
- Office staff just don't shove papers in the parents' faces; they speak to each individual by name.
- The receptionist calls ahead to remind patients of their upcoming office visit *and* so that the patients feel they have a relationship to the office.
- Dr. Fryer stops by the waiting room in between appointments to say hello to the families that are waiting.
- The doctor believes in really listening, and lets patients finish what they are saying before he speaks. He also lets children give their own histories. Children are graphic and descriptive, he finds, so once they are not afraid or put off, they really open up.
- Most practices have problems in bilingual situations, so Dr. Fryer has learned a second language: Spanish.

Dr. Fryer was fervent as he recounted this list of office policies. Serving his patients is something he believes in—and puts into practice. And being a technology fan, he recently made the move to connect online. You can find him on Twitter as @KidsHeartDoc.

Plenty of Places to Eat

I admit, I love to eat out, and I eat out a lot. I'll bet many of you do the same. We all have places where we go for takeout or a quick bite, and places where we go to have the complete dining experience.

Generally, we all tend to return to venues where we have a good time and are pleased with the service and food. We go to restaurants where we're comfortable, even if it's not a full-blown, fine-dining experience. My local Chinese takeout is my go-to place, because the food is well prepared. And the service? Well, let's just say they're polite. That's good enough for me when it comes to takeout.

There are other occasions when I like to be treated in a special manner. One of my go-to spots for that sort of experience is Craft Los Angeles. Aside from being the brainchild of Top Chef Tom Colicchio, the restaurant has an award-winning architectural design, incredibly attentive waiters, and unfussy, top-quality modern American cooking.

Whenever I make a reservation at Craft, they always ask for my cell number. Once I give them that, it's like they open a book: "How have you been, Ms. Collier? We haven't seen you for over a month!" Really? How do they know? I don't actually care— I'm sure they are using the restaurant version of Open Table Management Software. All I care about is that they make me feel like they really care about me, as a customer and a person.

Would you rather have 100 customers who visit once or 1 customer who visits 100 times? I would assume a loyal customer is more important.

Do you feel special when the chef, manager, or owner of a restaurant stops by your table? Most of us do. It's this kind of engagement that nets repeat visits and customer referrals. As a restaurateur, you benefit as well. Comments during these little customer chats may seem to be just small talk, but by proffering a little simple conversation you can gain insights into even minor things you're doing right or wrong. This should be your primary stealth customer research.

To gain customer loyalty, a restaurant might also include a comment card with the bill at the end of a meal. When I see one of these, I feel that the restaurant really cares what the customer thinks. These short forms generally ask questions about service, food quality, atmosphere, and value.

A really smart restaurateur also will provide an incentive for the customer to fill out the questionnaire, offering a discount for a future visit or a free small item, to encourage customers to give them this valuable feedback.

One more thing: Be sure when you solicit comments from customers that they believe you will pass along their feedback. It's all part of that mutual respect thing that makes people feel welcome.

Jeffrey J. Kingman (@JeffreyJKingman on Twitter) is CEO of Chalkboarder, a firm that provides international relationship engineering and strategic brand/concept development for the food industry. He mentioned that when customers don't fill out a card it's mainly because they think no one will pay attention to their comments. Jeff suggests that the server mention that the restaurant is "very interested in any comments about their visit," thereby giving customers verification that someone will actually read what they've written.

I recently lunched with a friend at a Los Angeles restaurant, Daily Grill in Studio City. The food was good, and the manager came around to inquire at the tables if everything was going well.

At the end of the meal, instead of the customer comment card, along with our bill came a form to join the restaurant's "Birthday Club." The deal was that if you joined the club, on your birthday you'd receive a voucher for $15 off a meal—with no expiration date! Not only did they get my contact information, but they piqued my interest as a customer.

If you have a restaurant, using customer comment cards, offering loyalty bonuses, making table visits, and keeping records on customers all will help you not only build up an e-mail list, but will go a long way toward building a community and list of possible places for improvement.

Even if you don't have a restaurant, there's a lot you can learn from restaurant best practices.

- *E-mail specials*: When I fill out the comment card at a restaurant that asks for my e-mail address, I get monthly updates and discount opportunities. Translate that to your business: Perhaps have a nice-looking guest book; or enclose a comment note along with your customers' receipts.
- *Social media outreach*: Include a field for your customers' Twitter ID, and ask whether they have a Facebook page; then "friend them" on both sites. Isn't it more personal to friend them than to ask them to join your fan page? That can come later.
- *Follow up.* Send an e-mail (or tweet them publicly) thanking your customers for their patronage. Let customers know you'd like to see them again. A public tweet shows the online community that you are there not only to promote your business, but to join in the conversation.

More to Photography Than Just Pictures

When was the last time you had a photo taken professionally? I mean a really good one. Okay, perhaps you've had your picture snapped at a local restaurant. Well, when someone who bills him- or herself as a photographer takes your picture, recognize there's a lot more to it than knowing the technical details of a camera.

Ever wonder what customer service skills a photographer needs? Aside from running a business and being nice to cus- tomers, expert photographers have to make their subjects feel comfortable. Uncomfortable people don't look their best in portraits.

In addition to having to learn the technical aspects of pho- tography and lighting, photographers must also be part artist, part psychic, and part politician. It takes a special kind of finesse and well-developed interpersonal skills to make people feel at ease when aiming a camera at them.

In a book called *Photographic Therapy*, author Rolando Gomez says that taking a good photo of a person can bolster his or her self-image and, perhaps, even change his or her life. Rolando is a Lexar Elite photographer, who, in 1999, transitioned from military combat photography to glamour photography, and still freelances as a photojournalist. He's known for his "flamour" (a contraction of *fashion* and *glamour*) style of photography. He has written five books and taught more than 400 workshops and seminars around the world.

In *Photographic Therapy*, he stresses that the subject's self- esteem is of utmost importance and that it's up to the photog- rapher to bolster it. If a subject feels that he or she is going to look good in a photo, that feeling will be reflected in the final image. Photographers shoulder that responsibility. They must have respect for their customers—true customer service.

Rolando photographs women from all walks of life, from famous authors and journalists to *Playboy* centerfolds. They all have one thing in common: They want to feel good about them- selves. (If you are interested in Rolando's book, *Photographic Therapy*, you can download it free on the Internet from www.freephotographybooks.com. Rolando is also on Twitter; connect with him, @RolandoGomez.)

Consider, too, the event photographer, the one who has to capture those special moments that flash by in an instant and may never come again. That's also quite a heavy burden to carry. How can these pros be sure to get their best shots?

I spoke to Josh Reiss, a Los Angeles-based photojournalist for *The LA Weekly* and the *Los Angeles Times*; he's also an event photographer. He takes pictures of everyone from celebrities to children; within that span comes a wide variety of personalities.

Many times at an event, under certain circumstances, people don't want to interact with photographers. This makes it tough to get the best shot, but as the photographer, that's the task at hand.

Josh works from a personal approach. "I like people," he says, "and find that if you treat them like people, you get back what you give." At family events and weddings, his goal is to be gracious and affable to all; and by the end of the event, he is often mistaken for one of the guests.

Photographing celebrities is a whole other story. In these cases, Josh feels that offering an honest, warm comment can engage the person enough to invoke the level of trust necessary to get the subject's cooperation. Too often, celebrity photographers just butt in and interrupt a conversation, to take their picture quickly. Josh takes a different spin: He first asks permission to take the photo, rather than just start shooting. The simple act of asking shows respect and gets him a lot more cooperation.

Sometimes the comment is as inconsequential as mentioning the celebrity's crazy travel or show schedule. Josh interacts with the individual as if he's talking to "another guy." Once the conversation starts, the photos become a joint venture—rather than one stranger taking pictures of another. The shoot then becomes a friendly exchange, rather than a dry business transaction.

"It's amazing how a simple, warm comment about the event or the work that they are doing will bring down a wall. When you're working with someone, everything is about your relationship with the person, [and] it will show up in the photo. I try to be personable; I'm able to relate to people 'on the go.'" Josh genuinely enjoys people, and when he relates with them, those interactions are projected into the photographs he takes.

Through his brief discussions with celebrities, Josh has been granted access to many shots because of the trust he builds during the brief time he spends with them. "My best photos come after I've struck up a conversation."

Josh also makes it easy for his clients to reach him on his Web site, www.CuriousJosh.com, or on Twitter as @CuriousJosh.

The challenges that these businesses face when dealing with customers are relevant to all businesspeople. If you apply the personal touch to the bulk of your interpersonal dealings, whether online or offline, your results will always be positive. Remember, customers are just people, who appreciate another human being taking the time to care about them and their needs.

There's a recurring theme here: The success a business earns is equal to the amount of thought it gives to the customer. No matter what the business, the customer, client, or patient needs to be treated like royalty.

3

Using Your Web Site to Connect with Your Customer

No matter how simple it may be, most businesses need a Web site. If you don't have a Web site, you should begin creating one today. If you do have a Web site, you are either selling your products or services there—or you're not. Being online (even if you're not selling products) is important so your prospective clients can get a clear picture of you, your staff, and your offerings.

If you're selling on the Web, your site is your home base for customer service connections. And since shoppers are notorious for abandoning orders pre-checkout, you must make sure you have done all you can to ensure that they click that Pay Now button. It's not just about offering quality merchandise; it's about establishing trust with, and inspiring confidence in, your buyers.

Here are a few things you should make sure to have on your Web site to help you gain your customers' trust:

- *Include a mailing address.* Web sites that do not include an address tend to look suspicious to prospective buyers. And, note, an actual address is often better than a post office box number. If you run your business from home and have security issues, you can always rent a mailbox at a UPS store or the like. This will give you a physical location to attach to your business name; and the reassurance that you work in a physical space really helps customers regard you as a reputable business.
- *Provide a phone number.* People like to know that they can reach a human being if they have a question on an item or a problem with an order. A Live Chat button is a nice addition for those who don't want to pick up a phone. (Don't forget to post the hours customers can reach someone through chat or phone.) More on how to set this up further on.
- *Include pertinent company information.* If yours is a family-run business, say so! Tell the background story of your company, and provide information about the people involved. Customers like doing business with individuals like themselves. Also, tell them you are focused on customer satisfaction.
- *Link to a page of frequently asked questions (FAQs).* Many Web shoppers have questions about the policies and logistics regarding how, when, and where you'll ship their purchase. Include information about your return policy as well, and whether you offer gift wrapping.
- *Feature testimonials from happy customers.* Including previous customers' positive comments on your site makes current and potential customers feel that they're in good company when they shop with you. Of course, to accomplish this, you need to . . .

- *Encourage customers to post reviews.* Many sites contain a special section for customer reviews. If that's too complex for your site, consider linking to a noncommerce site that posts product reviews for your industry. If, for example, you sell cameras, you might link to sites like www.ivillage.com, cnet .com, or steves-digicams.com, where your customers can read unbiased reviews of the experiences of others, then click back to your site to order from you. Keep in mind that while it's critical to allow customers to comment, you must be sure to moderate this feedback. Respond when necessary, and don't take negative remarks personally; simply try to view criticisms as suggestions for improvement.

Whether your online presence is an e-commerce site, a general site about your business, or a blog about what you do, you must *always* include a "Contact Us" or comment form. Do customers have the option of getting in touch with you in a variety of ways, beyond a phone number? Providing e-mail addresses and social media links are important, as well. Keep in mind there's a growing trend away from placing phone calls to companies, so show customers where they can reach you for swift attention when they want to solve a problem.

Web Site Alternative

If you're a professional who feels that having a Web site is not something you'd like to do, there is an alternative. You can have a Google profile. A Google profile can serve as your online resume or calling card—however you wish to format it. Anyone who searches your name on Google will find it on the

(continued)

(continued)

first page of search results. It features a "contact" link that, when clicked, opens an e-mail window and sends the resulting e-mail to a free Gmail account, which you can set up to forward directly to your computer's inbox.

Go to www.google.com/profiles and fill out the form; your profile will be live in moments. As a matter of fact, having a Google profile is important for anyone in business, as it gives people an alternate way to find and contact you. For an example, check out mine at www.google.com/profiles/marsha.collier.

When customers with an urgent issue want to get hold of you and can't, they may become frustrated and angry. Letting your customers know that they can reach you easily and in a variety of ways goes a long way toward preventing them from reaching the boiling point. Your prompt (as fast as possible) and courteous reply is what will save the day. You need your customers to have faith in your business. Part of establishing that faith is proving to them you are reliable, accessible, and responsive to their needs.

Be sure to classify queries by need when creating your Web site's contact form. This allows you to see at a glance, as you receive them, the issues that need an immediate response. It's easy to make a rule in your e-mail program that sorts your feedback responses by category, and routes them to separate mailboxes or folders.

Here's how it works for me: When an e-mail with specific words in the subject line arrives, it is immediately routed to separate folders in my inbox. I also route mail sent to specific e-mail addresses to a folder. (You can usually also set an alert to sound when one of these e-mails arrive.) I use Microsoft Office Outlook 2007, but I am sure if you're using a different e-mail program, the procedure will be similar.

Follow these steps to set up this function:

1. *Make new folders in your inbox for the various topics about which you might receive e-mail from your site.* For example, customer service, shipping, item questions, and any other appropriate titles—you know what's relevant to your business.
2. *Set the e-mail links on your site appropriately:* For example: customerservice@yoursite.com, shippinginquiries@yoursite .com, itemquestions@yoursite.com—again, whatever is applicable to your business.
3. *In the toolbar at the top of Outlook, click Tools.* (This will be slightly different if you're using another e-mail program.) Then select Rules and Alerts from the drop-down menu that appears, and the Rules and Alerts menu will appear. Mine is pictured in Figure 3.1, where you can see the e-mail folder routing I have set up.

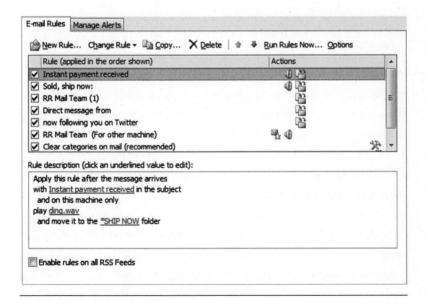

Figure 3.1   Setting up e-mail rules in Outlook.

4. *Click the New Rule tab to easily set up any number of rules.* This allows you to appropriately move your incoming e-mail to a folder that you will check regularly.

These customer e-mails should take priority over any others you receive, and should be answered as soon as possible. That is important.

Make sure, as well, that after customers click Leave Comment, they are taken to a page where you thank them for their time. You can set this up through a little form-forward that most hosting sites include in their packages. If you (or one of your employees) know a bit about HTML, it should be fairly easy to do. The resulting page should include a note from you to your customers that tells them how soon they can expect a response. (Be sure their comments are sent to the appropriate e-mail address you've set up in your e-mail software for flagging.)

If you can't answer e-mails immediately, at least arrange an auto-response. You can do this by installing a rule on your mail server or with your Internet service provider (ISP) that prompts your account to send out a response automatically, acknowledging that you've received the customers' e-mails. It's a good idea in the reply to let your customers know how much you care about their input, and give them an idea of how soon you will get back to them. Most importantly: Be sure you stick to this timeframe! Your timely response to any e-mail you receive communicates that attention is being paid to the customers, and that you respect their time and their business.

As your site gains traction on the Web, you might want to consider gathering e-mails for the purpose of marketing specials or to contact customers with service issues. Whatever your reason, compiling an e-mail list is worth its weight in gold. Keep in mind that proper Web etiquette says that you ask your customers to opt-in to your e-mail list. If you begin to bombard customers with mail they don't want, you may get a reputation as a spammer.

You might begin with a site like MailChimp.com, which also integrates with social media platforms. It offers a free starter account, which allows you to store up to 500 subscribers and send 3,000 e-mails a month. That's big enough to get a local business up and running at no extra cost.

Handling Those Urgent Messages

When was the last time you had to call your utility/insurance company, bank, or airline (fill in your personal favorite) and wasted precious minutes pressing numbers according to instructions—only to end up misdirected or, even worse, telling your story to one person who then has to switch you to someone else because it's "not my department"?

Interactive voice response (IVR)—or a *phone tree*, as it is more commonly known—is the interactive technology that allows a computer to detect voice and keypad inputs. If, on your Web site, you list a phone number as one of the best ways for your customers to contact you, be sure your phone system, voicemail, or phone tree is set up efficiently and effectively. If you have a phone call tree at your company (or if you're the only one answering—for now), it might be easier on you and your customers to point to an online live chat for e-commerce. Consider, for example, adding Live Chat to your site. There are plenty of software applications you can install to do this; further on, I give you some ideas.

Live Chat allows you or your employees to connect with your customers on the spot via voice or keyboarding. Customers can ask you their questions or describe their issues and be able to receive specific answers to their queries or concern. The program lets you easily connect, engage, and sell.

It is not necessary to shell out hundreds of dollars at the outset of your business for anything but equipment and merchandise that are absolutely essential. So how can you handle a live chat for your customers? There are quite a few options for you before you hit the big time.

Skype

This is the ideal entry-level method for your business to use to engage in interactive customer chat. Skype places free calls from computer to computer and, for a small fee, will forward incoming calls to your landline or cell phone.

When you sign up for a Skype account, you have the option of using professional-looking buttons and/or easily customized widgets that you can install anywhere and everywhere on your site. Once these icons are on your Web pages, all your customer needs to do is click, and Skype will ring you at your computer and allow you to talk live.

Providing that extra level of customer service via person-to-person, live-voice interaction will save many a sale. It also gives you the opportunity to negotiate, up-sell, or add a personal touch to transactions. If a customer is making a large purchase, for example, offer him or her discounts or sale prices on related items (Victoria's Secret operators do this very successfully). Your customers can contact you through their computer microphone and speakers to yours at no cost to you. You can also opt to have Skype forward incoming calls to your home or cell phone when you're away.

An additional option available from Skype is to purchase Skype-enabled telephones that use your home office/home wireless internet to connect directly to the service. You can also download a Skype application to your smartphone, enabling you to make and receive Skype calls. (It's available on many platforms;

check your app store.) This eliminates the need to run back to your computer to answer every query. If you're considering putting chat on your site, keep in mind that you must ensure that someone will be present when a chat request comes in. If you don't offer 24/7 service, be sure to indicate which hours chat is available and include an e-mail address where off-hour queries may be sent.

Meebo Me

Meebo Me is a free, simple widget that you can insert into any Web site quickly and easily. It will work on any Web page where you can embed HTML and a flash widget (including most blogging platforms). It enables you to set your status to display whether you are online or offline; if you are offline, visitors can leave you a message that you can respond to when you return to your computer.

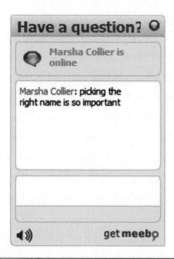

Figure 3.2 Handle questions from customers quickly with Meebo.

Java-Based Chat

When building your site, you can also install one of the many free Java applets available on the Web—like Google Live Chat or chatapplet.net. These tiny pieces of code put up a real chat service on your site, an economical option for companies that are just starting out. If you're the slightest bit handy with your Web site, you can simply install a Java-based applet to present a professional-looking, Live Chat window where you and your customers can type back and forth. If you don't want to attempt this yourself, ask your Webmaster—or even the high school kid next door—to install it for you.

Live Chat Software

This is the next step up for most online entrepreneurs. Once your budget is in place, you can install a personalized Live Chat program on your site. You might be amazed to learn that a top-drawer Live Chat program can be had for as little as $99 a year and that you can customize and tailor it to your company's needs. Software like this is available from providers such as providesupport.com, whose tool allows you to handle multiple chats at the same time and customize everything from graphics to the form your customer sees on the screen.

You or your employee(s) can leave the window open on your computers; this way, whenever a question comes in, you can respond tout de suite. When Zappos' Tony Hseih was at LinkExchange, for example, he and his partner would drop everything to respond to a customer query. You can offer that level of top-quality service, too.

You can also monitor visitors to your site in real time by seeing which items they're checking out, how long they're spending on the page, and where they are from. Information like this will help you further customize your product offerings and descriptions to attract a larger customer base.

Live Chat Hosted Solutions

For about the same price as Live Chat software, you can install a hosted solution, which simplifies the installation process. When you sign up with one of these services, you get a small piece of code to insert on your Web page. The software's actual mechanism resides on a computer out on the Web tubes at a far-off, secure server farm. They maintain the software so you don't have to.

One of the many available hosted services is live2support .com. This site offers a browser-based interface and a stand-alone that can run as an independent program on your computer. A hosted solution saves you from having to worry about bandwidth issues, and the stand-alone browser-independent versions will save considerably on your system resources.

Outsourced Chat

When your e-commerce site starts pulling in some big money every month—or if your customers are coming in from all over the world, and you don't want to miss the call from a shopper who's 10 time zones away—it may be time to consider outsourcing your live chat. You never know: That guy from Dubai might place a really big order, but he has one little question and your answer could put his buying decision over the top.

Perhaps your budget is still a little tight, though. If you're not ready to hire someone across the world full-time, check out services like those offered by g5live.com. This site allows small- to medium-sized companies to provide 24/7 outsourced service on a per-call basis. For $2.95 a call, you can have someone to answer that question from your potential big spender in Dubai.

Outsourcing may well be a better solution than leaving your prospective customers unattended at those times when you're not around. But first ask yourself whether this is something you really want to do: Will you be sacrificing your direct connection to your customers?

To that end, you might want to consider the possibility of having *two* chat links for your customers: an outsourced platform for when you are out and about and enjoying life, and an online direct chat with you or your employees during business hours.

Keep in mind the reason you took your business online. Was it to enable customers from all over the world to find your store at any time on any day? If that is the case, then be true to your mission. Do the best job you can to engage and connect with your customers everywhere, at every possible level.

Explain Products and Services with Videos

YouTube is an entertaining and easy-to-use site that gives you an opportunity to reach your customers via video. Millions of people watch videos on YouTube.com every day; all you need to start making your own is some good lighting and a video camera. The best tactic here is to produce short videos on topics that relate to your business then upload them to YouTube and link to your Web site or blog.

Let's say, for example, that you're a certified public accountant (CPA): You can make a video to remind your clients about tax deadlines, or provide tips on how to organize receipts and keep the books. If you're a beauty salon owner, you can post some hair-care how-to videos. And a pharmacist—well, how about home safety and drug tips? If you manufacture a product, you can demonstrate how to use it in a video; or show how to perform maintenance on it, or make small repairs. You're limited only by your imagination.

One way to get started is to think about the questions you've been asked in the past about your company, products, and/or services, and turn the answers into a video. People are always asking you questions, right? Make note of the most frequently asked ones, and you'll soon have your own series.

Take John Lawson (@ColderICE on Twitter), eBay and online entrepreneur: He decided to produce a simple video, "How to Fold a Bandana," to promote sales for his Web site, 3rdpower outlet.com. Posted on YouTube, the video at the time of this writing had 143,601 views. John doesn't sell a thing in the video; it's merely a demonstration of how to use one of his products. His sales of bandanas now have exceeded 11,000 units. He says this is directly attributable to the video.

Some tips for making your video:

- *It's best to have someone else help you.* That way, you can loosen up prior to shooting, and the assistant can act as both your audience and videographer. If not, a tripod works in a pinch.
- *Look in the mirror before you begin.* Be sure your appearance befits the profession you represent. Image is everything— *especially* in a video!
- *Use a high-definition (HD) camera, if possible.* People are getting used to seeing things on the Web in crystal-clear resolution; you don't want to look fuzzy or outdated.
- *Check the lighting.* Be sure there are no unflattering shadows on you or your product.
- *Be sure your background is clean and neat.* Nothing is more distracting in a video or photo than messy surroundings.
- *Use a free shareware program to edit and insert a professional title.* I use Microsoft Windows Movie Maker; it is free with your Windows operating system and is very easy to use. Quicktime Pro is a low cost solution for Apple users.

- *Keep your video brief.* Compose and edit what you plan to say *before* you go on camera. We live in a short-attention-span era in which people will turn you off if they don't get the message quickly and succinctly.

If you want to see some of the videos I uploaded for my eBay book audience, search my name on YouTube, or find me by my username, DealingDiva.

4

Developing a Blog to Engage Customers

Web sites have become de rigueur for any type of business. Since your customers are on the Web—and because your competitors have a presence there—you must have one, too.

But what happens when you want to go beyond a simple Web site? When you feel you're ready to take the next step, you can develop a blog to connect with customers. Blogs provide a place for you to enhance your company's messages and policies in an editorial style, as well as respond to readers' comments.

The word *blog* is merely a contraction of the words *web* and *log*. A blog can be a commentary, as in print journals, or a description of events. When the "blogosphere" first came into being, the individuals engaging in this activity were considered to be "journaling" on the Web. They spoke of their daily events and families; soon enough, these home journalists became known as *bloggers*. The transition from individual to business blog use morphed very quickly, because a business can integrate its messages into an interaction with its customers.

Though their importance is increasingly evident to big business, a 2009 University of Massachusetts study, "The Fortune 500 and Social Media: A Longitudinal Study of Blogging and Twitter Usage by America's Largest Companies," found that only 108 (22 percent) of Fortune 500 companies were actively running a blog. Of those 108 corporate blogs, 93 (86 percent) linked to active Twitter accounts (three times more than the previous year's study). Active Twitter accounts for the Fortune 500 (those who posted within the 30 days prior to the study), only totaled 173. It is also interesting to note that when the university surveyed *Inc.* 500 companies, it found that they were earlier and more vigorous adopters, with 45 percent having a blog. It will be interesting to see the changes in their annual research.

If you are thinking of creating a blog, just remember: If you can't do it right, don't do it at all. A blog requires a significant investment of time, as well as frequent and consistent updating. And although a blog can be a low-cost alternative to a Web site, do yourself a favor: Create a quality Web site for your business first. If you want to have a blog, too, make sure it is linked several places from within your company site.

Your e-commerce or business Web site is a *must*; a blog is an option. There are many other new tools with which to micro-blog or to connect, without sustaining a constant stream of company news.

Running a small entrepreneurial enterprise gives you a leg up on big business. You can move faster and make changes on the fly. There are more than 150 million blogs on the Internet these days, read by approximately 400 million people worldwide. That's a lot of blogs, and a lot of people spending time online.

How can you make yours different from all the rest? What would you say if you were to start a blog about your business?

What information could you give beyond the usual material regarding the progress and changes occurring in your business or industry?

Well, you could talk about sales and new ideas, and get your customers' opinions on them. But do your customers have the time to read your blog? And are you committed enough to write one on a regular basis? A business blog that only posts occasionally can get very stale in a hurry.

All that said, blogs are a great idea, and if you have someone in your business who can handle additional posting responsibilities, congrats! Just be aware, as in all social media, you can't just turn the blog duties over to an intern or that college kid you hired. It has to be written by someone who is deeply invested in the direction your business is taking. The responsibility most frequently falls on the entrepreneur.

To blog successfully, you must be prepared to:

1. Enjoy writing—or at the very least, researching the Web for tidbits to share about your industry.
2. Have a good command of the English language and grammar.
3. Devote scheduled time to produce your blog.
4. Maintain a level of excitement and interest for your readers.
5. Be prepared to post at least five to six times a month.
6. Respond to comments posted on your blog to start up the conversation.

As with all social media, the blogger needs to be you, a respected employee, or even a family member. Whoever you choose must have free time to respond to comments; as important, you must be comfortable that the message he or she is sending reflects exactly what you would say yourself. At the same time, letting employees think outside the box, and backing them up when they do, should be part of your company culture.

The push for companies to blog is a recent trend in business; it is a wonderful way to connect with customers. If you're wondering how and where to start, it's always a good idea to remember to start small until you get the hang of it (once you've decided blogging is for you).

Blogs can be geared to any interest imaginable. They can target specific interests and hobbies, become a voice to the customer, or be designed for the benefit of other businesses. One my favorite small business blogs is SmallBizSurvival.com, where Becky McCray doses out words of wisdom for rural small businesses. She also writes a blog for her own liquor store at allensretail.com. Her retail blog is filled with interesting facts and tips about her products.

Her advice for small businesspeople interested in writing a blog is: "Write down every basic question a customer asks you. Start today, and do this for two weeks. If you end up with a long list of questions you can answer, then you have enough material to start a blog." Combine those questions with information about your products, and you'll have the beginnings of your own commercial blog.

Becky adds, "The one *big* secret to making [a blog] work? Focus on what *customers* want to know, not what you want to tell them, about your business."

Engaging with Your Brand on Your Blog

Once you've established a well-run, quality Web site, you can use a blog to improve the site's overall organic search rankings. It may also allow you to brand yourself as an expert in your industry. Bottom line: Have a plan and an objective to focus on before you start writing your blog topics.

The following guidelines may help you decide whether or not it's time for you to launch a blog:

1. *Post regularly.* Ideally, you should make an entry at least two to three times per week. Blogging, as I said, needs to be done on a regular basis.

2. *Provide quality content.* Your blog will not draw views if it merely provides a constant stream of what you do or your company does. The goal is to engage the reader's interest, so don't just write about business; write about topics that you enjoy. This way, your posts will offer useful information and let readers and customers know about your passions. Target your posts to your readers as well, and write about subjects they find interesting. If you desire, hone the focus to a narrow niche of broader-interest topics. This ensures that you won't run out of new things to say.

3. *Post current customer service issues.* Are your shipments being delayed by a snowstorm or floods? Is there a problem with one of your products that an employee or customer discovered? Your blog is the place to let your customers know about these matters, and provide them aid in dealing with them.

4. *Answer comments.* If your readers post comments on your blog, be sure to respond. Address everything—negative and positive. Don't let anything remain on the blog unanswered for days.

5. *Be transparent.* The old-school customer service tactic was to send out press releases. Today's customers prefer to be part of the conversation. Don't fake positive comments on the blog. As the owner of your business, you are a reflection of your company. Always speak from your own point of view. Be available, honest, and understanding.

Keep in mind that for your blog to be a valuable resource for your business, and worth your time and effort, your customers need to visit and actually read it. There are countless blogs that receive just a few hits a day; if your customers are busy, a marketing-oriented blog may be the last place they want to visit. If, on the other hand, your content has the slightest relevance to them, the more Web-savvy visitors may subscribe to the Really Simple Syndication (RSS) stream and read it when new items are posted.

I keep my blog updated randomly, mainly because I'm active on various other sites across the Web. When I do update, I do so only with content that I feel will be of interest to my readers. I've found that this approach works for me as a brand. Aside from business ideas, I often post from a personal point of view. People seem to like it; they subscribe and comment often. Find the approach that works best for you by monitoring visitors using a service like Feedburner.com. In this way, you'll be able to see which posts on your blog get the most views, thereby enabling you to tailor future posts to that particular area of interest.

As a small businessperson, you may find that you have no time to spare for keeping a blog up to date. In short: If you don't think you have the time to dedicate to a blog now, remember that you can do so later.

Reposting the Good Stuff on Posterous

As Web development moves faster, things are getting simpler. One site, www.posterous.com, makes it simple to blog your own ideas, plus share content from other sites on your own personal page. What could be easier? When you find information that's interesting and related to your business, you can place it on your Posterous page. It's blogging for nonbloggers. You can either post from the Web, or simply e-mail your content and photos. It's just that easy.

A quick idea can be written and posted directly from your smart-phone, should you have relevant information to share. Write the occasional post on material from your specific industry. If you're a CPA, for example, you can write your own story and link to great articles from the Web on taxes. Posterous allows you to add lots of content easily and keep the page fresh and engaging.

As I said, the process is simple, enabling you to instantly connect to people with all your Web e-mail addresses (Gmail, Hotmail, AOL mail, and Yahoo! mail). With a few clicks of a button, you can invite a good base of people to visit your Posterous page. Building your page takes virtually no time at all. To set it up, go to www.posterous.com and take the following steps:

1. *Register and select a theme, which you can customize with your brand colors.* You can make the theme as basic or complex as you wish. The site has pretty decent templates, or you can easily customize a theme to your liking.
2. *Select your site address (mine is marshacollier.posterous.com) that will readily identify you or your business.* You can give your Posterous page a custom domain (instructions are on the site) once you're comfortable using the site.
3. *Download the Bookmarklet, a small applet that you drag from the Posterous site to your browser's Bookmark bar.* When you come across some information you'd like to share, the program enables you to just click the Post to Posterous button and set up the content you wish to share.
4. *Autopost.* Set up Posterous to cross-post your content to Twitter, Facebook, your blog, or almost any social media site on the Web. Keep in mind that repetition isn't always the best idea. Each platform has a certain audience, and not all posts are appropriate for each group, so don't set up Posterous to broadcast everywhere blindly.

What makes all of this so exciting is that we are all sharing and commenting and engaging, while constantly meeting new people and businesses. If you want to check out someone who really knows about serious business blogs, visit MackCollier.com. Mack knows his stuff when it comes to blogs. (By the way: no relation.)

Some Regulations Apply

Although many of the technologies and tools we use today to promote or connect in our businesses are referred to collectively as *new media*, they are also considered advertising—*creative* advertising, at that. As such, any use of the Internet to market your business may by governed by any number of rules, even federal regulations.

Whether it's a blog, a tweet, or your Facebook page—or whatever the new shiny tool is tomorrow—any message you broadcast to the public will fall under the regulatory guidelines of the Federal Trade Commission (FTC) concerning the use of endorsements and testimonials in advertising. The FTC came up with some spanking new guidelines to cover new media, as of December 1, 2009, a few of which you should keep close to your heart:

1. The material connection between advertiser and endorser should be disclosed in the advertisement.
2. Advertisers using blog advertising can be held liable for bloggers' statements. (This applies when you send samples to a blogger in exchange for a write-up.)
3. Endorsers must remain a user of the product or service during the run of the advertisement. For example, does Brooke Shields really use Latisse? You bet—at least she did during the run of her commercials for the product.

Before you make an expensive mistake, check out the full text of the FTC's ruling at: www.ftc.gov/os/2009/10/091005endorsementguidesfnnotice.pdf. Though these guidelines technically are not legally binding, they do provide a foundation that you can use in order to protect against liability. Odds are that a violation will net you a cease-and-desist notice; and, typically, only fines are used as a way to deter and punish repeat offenders. Fines are rumored to be up to $11,000.

Got a Brick-and-Mortar Location?

If your business has a retail location, there are a couple more "musts" to know about regarding your customer service outreach. There is a growing number of Web sites that aggregate their user-generated evaluations of real-world businesses. Each site is a community of its own, often with vociferous and savvy users. Customer service—along with quality of product—is the buzzword on these sites. Businesses that have their fingers on the pulse of social media monitor their listings on these sites. This allows them to quickly catch if and when a negative review has been posted and address it immediately. These sites let you read reviews of your business, respond, and solve a problem before your listing—and reputation—can be damaged any further. Chapter 7 goes into more specifics on handling your outreach on these sites.

5

Connecting with Your Customers Where They Play

When your customers are spending social time on the Web (on their computers or their phones), they are open to interacting with you, as well as their friends. This is your opportunity to participate in social sites to reach them. These sites are an extension of your community outreach, an important part of your online customer service plans. Building a community will help you grow a positive reputation—and there's nothing like social networking for building community.

Your community on these sites will grow slowly; but if you work them, it *will* work for you. In time, you will have a solid group of people who will see your announcements (marketing messages) interspersed among your interesting content. Again, your company is building a friendly business relationship through social networking.

You don't have a legal department to approve your project, just your common sense. So why not read on and dive in?

Making Fans on Facebook

You *are* on Facebook, aren't you? It's not just for socializing, you know. Lots of busy businesspeople are checking this site, where they answer customer service queries as well as keep up with friends and family. Facebook is all about community; your kids are there, right along with your parents. (The fastest-growing demographic on Facebook is over 35, so if that's your market, this is a good place to reach them.)

Facebook has grown to more than 500 million users. The average user spends 55 minutes per day on the site, and big business is slowly finding its way there as well. Aside from the personal pages we all know and love, Facebook's feature for businesses is called a *fan page*. Figure 5.1 shows a fan page for a family-run company that uses the site to get its message out and link to its Web site.

Facebook is more of a brand-building, community-fostering venue than a forum for dealing with customer service issues instantaneously. The responses remain on the page permanently—and don't move along in a stream as they do on Twitter—which means both the good and bad stuff can stick like glue.

Both big brands and small businesses can foster not only brand building, but brand improvement, as well, by reading what their customers post on their pages. There may be product suggestions or comments about service received; all are worth a reply, not to mention serious consideration by your planning team.

I visited the company pages of a few businesses that are highly regarded for their social media outreach. Smack dab on one big brand's page I found several unanswered nasty customer service issues. It was somewhat surprising to the commenting community

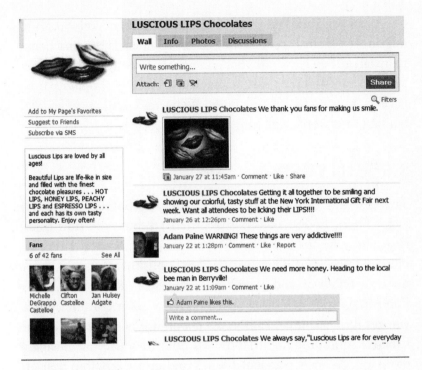

Figure 5.1   Small businesses can easily create their own communities.

that a company with such a famous reputation for "reaching out" gave no reply. This is a testament to the fact that if you have a social media outreach program, you'd best stay on top of it and monitor comments.

Your Facebook business page should provide information on your products, industry, and customers, and display your own announcements. You can respond to any touchy remarks left by your fans by clicking the commenter's name and sending him or her a private message. But Facebook's primary purpose is to enable you to engage with your customers openly, through your posts and content and by replying to members.

As I write this, Facebook is enabling Amazon Web Stores to sell directly from Facebook Fan pages. Pampers is the first brand to install a "Buy Now" tab that connects directly to their Amazon Web store. Whether customers will embrace shopping from Facebook, or prefer visiting brand Web sites is still an unknown, but an event worth watching.

Setting Up Your Pages

The best way to start on Facebook is by setting up a personal page. There are lots of books out there to show you how to do this; pick one up to make the process go smoother. I recommend *Facebook For Dummies* (Wiley Publishing, Inc., 2008) or my own *Facebook and Twitter For Seniors For Dummies* (Wiley Publishing, Inc., 2010), for the brevity of their content. Once you get into the swing of how Facebook works, and have established a solid group of friends, it's time to start your business fan page. As your personal friends and customers join you on your personal page, you can invite them to become fans of your company page.

The ease with which you can use Facebook is amazing. You can comment on a friend's post, upload a photo, update your status, or, if you're not in a chatty state of mind, click the Like link next to a friend's post. Your visit becomes a part of the page for all to see.

Begin by offering friendship to anyone you know, and who knows your business. You'll be surprised how many people will find you, in turn. Your list of Facebook friends can become the basis for your business fan page. However, don't feel bad if some of your personal Facebook friends don't join your business fan page. They may not be familiar with your business, and until they are, they might not be interested in becoming fans.

I'm both a brand and a small business, so I have two pages on Facebook. My personal page is at www.facebook.com/marsha .collier, and my fan page is at www.facebook.com/MarshaCollier FanPage. Take a look at them both for a moment and notice the differences. When you friend me on my personal page, you'll be able to see what I'm doing, where I'm going, and which charities I post about, and get to know my friends. When you friend me, I can also send you an invitation to join my fan page.

My fan page has more of my business information: books I'm writing, industry articles, and places I'm appearing. Your fan page can show new items, photos of your customers (also friends on Facebook), articles from the Web that focus on your area of expertise, links to posts from your blog, and any updates to information on your store or company. A secondary benefit of a fan page is that you can "crowd source" (ask open questions) your fans and get answers that can help you mold and change your business.

As a small business owner, you can use Facebook to build a community and interact personally with your customers and clients. Figure 5.2 is an example of the boarding facility that I use for my cats when I'm traveling. It does a great job of building both a community and its client base through its business page.

By commenting on Facebook friends' pages, you can encourage their friends to join yours, too. Be sure to participate with your page fans by visiting their personal pages and clicking Like on a post here and there, as you do on your personal page. You want to be involved with your fans on a personal level.

You don't have to have thousands of fans or followers for your page to succeed. Remember, quality, not quantity. Your business goal is to connect with prospective and/or current customers. Once you start, be sure to promote the fact that you're on Facebook at your physical location, if you have one. Putting a small sign at your reception desk will inform customers about

Figure 5.2 Note how the California Cat Center involves its friends on the page.

your page on Facebook and encourage them to sign up once they get home. Los Angeles–based Western Bagel takes this kind of promotion seriously, as you can see in Figure 5.3.

Once you've set up your fan page, fill it with various news bits on a regular basis, such as:

- Links to stories you've found on the Web that relate to your field.
- Information about new company features.
- Links to new elements of your Web site or blog.
- New product or service innovations from your business.

Figure 5.3   You can't miss this billboard-size display.

- Information from your Posterous page (you can set up Posterous to automatically update your Facebook when you post there).
- Notices of special sales and discounts.
- New customer welcomes, birthday wishes and other personal touches.
- Responses to customer messages; compliments and complaints.

You'll want to use marketing updates on your fan page sparingly, since social media is about relationship marketing, not direct selling. Your community members won't hang around long if you are constantly hammering them on the head with sales messages. Rather, they're apt to feel used, and abandon your page.

Should you have Internet sales, or want to reach more people in your geographic area, you can build your audience (and future customer base) by purchasing ads for your page on Facebook. This is a way to draw attention to your page and to bring in fans. It's difficult to handle customer service online if no one knows you have a page on Facebook. An ad with an eye-catching title may engage people who have never heard of you (or your business) before.

Setting up an ad for your page requires a bit of thought, however. The questions that Facebook asks users upon their initial registration give the site a clear picture of who its members are. You will rarely see such specific demographic filtering available on any site, much less a social site. If, say, you rent tuxedos or own a bar, you could target your fan page ad to singles in a particular age group.

There are 10 targeting factors available for your ad, some—or all—of which you can define:

- *Location.* If you have only one location, Facebook can stipulate that your ad appear only on the pages of users who live in your own city or state. If yours is a Web-based business, on the other hand, you can send the ad to the entire United States; and if you cater to buyers from foreign countries, you can also target them.
- *Age.* No big secret here. If you're marketing to teens, select the age range you want to direct your ad.
- *Sex.* You'll want to check on this if your service or product is gender-specific.
- *Relationships.* Are your target customers single? In a relationship? Married? Here's where you can find them.
- *Interested In.* This tells you where your fans romantic interests lie—ideal if you offer items for gift-giving or holidays.

- *Education*. If you want to target a specific level of education, you may do so here.
- *Birthday*. Want your ad to be seen on someone's birthday? Just indicate this, and offer a small gift or discount at your store or business.
- *Workplaces*. Use this filter to build awareness in specific organizations.
- *Connections*. This allows you to include and exclude users based on the pages, events, and applications they have joined/attended/liked.
- *Keywords*. People are asked to indicate their interests, so if, for example, you're looking for fitness fiends, *Star Trek* fans, or equestrians, you can steer the message via keywords.

You can also feature an image of one of your customers or page fans in the ad (be sure to ask permission first). This can add a personal touch to your ads. I lent my image to a Web site, SingularCity.com, which ran the ad shown in Figure 5.4 on Facebook. The ad was targeted to Los Angeles singles.

**Best in LA –
SingularCity**

Marsha Collier, famous
author of eBay for
Dummies series is a
Member of SingularCity.
Join successful singles
in LA: FREE Membership.

Figure 5.4 My image on an ad for SingularCity.com, which ran on Facebook.

A word about targeting: You run the risk of limiting the reach of your message if you cast your ads narrowly, and might not get as much cluck for your buck. Since Facebook lets you change your targeting on the fly, visit the stats page and see what is working. You can continue tinkering until you've found just the right group for your message.

I've learned from experience that even after you think you've identified your target market, it can shift at the blink of an eye. The Internet is a moving target; trends and preferences change quickly. So keep tweaking the ad and its content to build your community.

Establishing the base for an online following makes it easier— and a whole lot more fun—to service your customers. Your community will provide you with influencers, who will spread your message outside the circle.

Geolocation Services: Foursquare and Whrrl

There are some sites that, unlike Facebook, are more applicable to people using mobile devices. These sites—whose numbers are growing—reward their users for checking in from their smartphones when they are out and about. Two of these are Foursquare .com and Whrrl.com. The mobile "checking in" activity is getting more and more popular with folks who connect online. Most social geolocating services work in a similar fashion, and the tactics you use for Foursquare can be used with all of them.

When users check in at these sites, their friends can see where they are. Repeat visits earn users badges of honor and place them higher in an internal ranking system.

All of this is done via a game mechanic: Users earn points, win "mayorships," and unlock badges for trying new places and revisiting old favorites.

Foursquare allows the user to become the "mayor" of a business or spot he or she frequents by being the person who checks in at a single location most often. (The associated title in Whrrl Societies is a "Changemaker.") This high status is coveted by players of these games; and when someone gets ousted, there's usually a scramble to reinstate him or her as the mayor again by a repeat visit.

I suspect that most company Web sites will be joining the location game. In June 2010, the *Wall Street Journal*'s Web site became the first to experiment with an "Add to Foursquare" button. So if you're reading a restaurant review or other cultural coverage on WSJ.com, you'll be able to click a button to add the venue(s) mentioned in the article to your Foursquare to-do list, along with a tip written by a WSJ editor that link backs to the original article.

How does this translate into developing a loyal online customer service community? Smart businesses take advantage of this titular status by offering discounts and bonuses to mayors and repeat visitors. Some offerings include free French fries or desserts with a meal, and various discounts promoted in restaurants and clubs. A crafty idea might be to speed up some of your slower business hours with a special, such as: "Check in between 4:00 and 6:00 PM for a free draft beer." You can easily promote this on your Web site, Facebook, or Twitter, or you can have Foursquare or Whrrl do it for you.

Whrrl launched its Society Rewards program with a promotion for Murphy USA (@Murphy_USA), a gasoline and convenience store with more than 1,000 locations throughout the United States. Whrrl users who checked in at Murphy's stations won a bevy of ongoing prizes—most notably, one daily winner was awarded a digital coupon for $50 in free gas.

If you register your business to be eligible for Foursquare's "mayoral" discount, the smartphone mobile application will notify the Mayor of the discount whenever he or she checks in from your location. To "claim your business" on

Foursquare to offer mobile specials, go to http://foursquare.com/
businesses. Once you register your business, you gain access to a
set of tools that easily enable your offerings. Currently, the tools
allow for the following automatic awards (be on the lookout for
more):

- *Mayor specials.* Specials that can be unlocked only by the current mayor.
- *Check-in specials.* Awarded when a customer checks in a prescribed number of times.
- *Frequency specials.* Repeat visits are awarded on a regular schedule that you specify—say, every 5 or 10 visits.
- *Wildcard specials.* These are always unlocked, but have conditions that must be verified by a member of your staff (e.g., "Show us your JetSetter badge and get a free coffee").

Your special will not only show up on Foursquare, but you
are free to advertise with downloadable graphics available on the
site. Also, with a few clicks of your mouse, you can promote
the special on your Facebook page, or tweet it to your followers.
Figure 5.5 shows how the Hyatt Regency Tampa is promoting a
Foursquare deal to its followers on Twitter. (See how social networking ties it all together)?

If someone checks in at a location near your business, he or
she may receive a notification that there is a mayor discount
or check-in discount nearby awaiting the visitor if he or she
chooses to stop by your location.

Visitors to your site don't have to become mayor to receive
a special offer from you, either; you can provide a Foursquare
check-in special. Kate Spade's 65 New York boutiques recently
offered this deal: "Hello sunshine! Enjoy 15 percent off full-priced

Figure 5.5   That's good incentive to become mayor.

merchandise when you check in to our shop. Looking to get away? Enter for a chance to win an escape to Bali inside. Offer ends 6/21/10."

Other major players have been parlaying the service/marketing slant of these games. Starbucks, for example, offers a "Barista" badge to frequent customers who attain a prescribed number of check-ins at a Starbucks location. Currently, the company is even toying with the idea of tying the badge and number of check-ins to an in-store rewards program. Not a bad idea to emulate!

Remember that although this all seems like fun and games, it can have a serious influence on how often these game-players frequent your business.

Sign up for these geolocation sites at their business portals:

- http://rewards.whrrl.com
- http://foursquare.com/signup_specials

Joining in where your customers play online is a highly effective (and unobtrusive) way to build community with your customers, via a very simple and localized campaign.

6

Microblogging for Service, Fun, and Profit

Initially on the Web, people started to journal, which evolved into blogging; then miniblogs (with shortened posts) became popular; and now there's microblogging. A microblog is a platform set up to accept posts that are only a sentence or so in length. Perhaps even only a sentence fragment, a video, or a photo will be posted. Microblogging is generally thought to have come about via the popularization of chat, instant, and text messaging. The most popular microblog these days is Twitter; it's become the platform upon which the rules of microblogging are constantly being made and broken. What we learn on Twitter will lay the foundation for reaching out to customers on future forms of online social media. Early adopters arrived, followed by major companies, which are finding value in reaching out to customers there.

Twitter is unquestionably the simplest and most convenient format to make your online customer connections. Do you send text messages from your phone? If so, you're given room for 160 characters—20 more than Twitter allows. You can run your Twitter communications from your computer, or on your smartphone if you wish. Admittedly, getting your point across in 140 characters *is* a challenge; it often takes me a lot of editing. However, once you get the hang of short messaging, it can become second nature.

Some quick Twitter stats as of April 2010:

- There are an estimated 105,779,710 registered users on the site.
- New users sign up at the rate of 300,000 per day.
- Each month, 180 million unique visitors come to the site.
- Total daily tweets average 55 million.

From its recent humble beginnings, Twitter has been launched into the top 10 Web sites in the United States (as rated by alexa.com)—alongside eBay, Google, Wikipedia, and Amazon. Currently, its longest reach is among Web denizens under 45; but it will surely catch up with Facebook and reach the older crowd shortly.

At first blush, what we as entrepreneurs can gain from Twitter is a window into our customers' daily lives. Twitter gives us the ability to monitor comments made about our businesses, as well as to get our messages out in a friendly, nonconfrontational manner.

Microblogging on Twitter is truly a realm in which one loud voice from a satisfied customer can reach millions of ears and spread news worldwide. With equal power, a single unhappy voice can damage a business reputation with lightning speed. There are several sites where you can visualize the reach of one powerful Twitter voice. Make a visit to www.TwitterAnalyzer.com and input the Twitter ID of a brand you know on the home page. I checked a popular brand, Coca-Cola; its tweets on the day I looked had reached a massive 1,376,960 people. TwitterAnalyzer calculates Reader Reach and Unique Readers Reach based on the number of people following a Twitter ID. This estimates the number of eyes exposed to a message on any particular day.

Reaching the customer "where they live" is what it's all about. The big guys have all gotten a positive spin from their communications on Twitter: @Zappos, @Starbucks, @DellOutlet, @ComcastCares, @CocaCola; politicians @BarackObama, @Sen JohnMcCain, @SenChrisDodd, @RussFeingold, @SarahPalin USA, and @NewtGingrich; even celebrity brands like @aplusk (Ashton Kutcher) and @BritneySpears.

A unique example of the latter is @KathyIreland. Well known as a supermodel, she has parlayed her business savvy into a major enterprise. She founded Kathy Ireland Worldwide, and by 2005 it had generated $1.4 billion in sales. You can't do that with just a pretty face; you get there by working hard, and Kathy knows how to relate to people and is very active on Twitter, personally tweeting regularly from her account. She talks to her fans, customers, and readers of her books from all corners of the planet. When Kathy was volunteering in Haiti after the earthquake, she tweeted about her experiences there, and her followers hung on her words.

Not only does Kathy tweet, she talks to people. She listens to their problems and offers sympathetic advice. She hears about illnesses and offers prayers for the families. She talks about them, wishes them happy Mother's Day, happy birthday, happy graduation. She is part of her fans' online families. She puts a human face on big business.

These brands use participation, transparency, and caring to connect with their customers. Likewise, people who follow your business on Twitter will be able to see your levels of communication with your customers and friends. (The only possible fly in the ointment is whether you can back up your positive public spin with good, old-fashioned quality service and products.)

Before you get involved on Twitter, ask yourself some questions: Are you good at conversing with people? Can you stifle your anger when someone makes a rash comment, and come up with a positive answer instead? If so, Twitter is an excellent place to begin your customer service campaign.

Here are some of the pluses a Twitter account can add to your business:

- Help you organize "tweetups"—live events that you sponsor for your Twitter followers and local community—in a short period of time.
- Provide you with search and numerous other tools to monitor your account, enabling you to see what people are saying about you.
- Give you the opportunity to respond publicly to customer queries and questions.
- Show that your business is run by people, that it's not just a cold, hard enterprise.
- Help you spread the word easily if you are supporting a charity or cause.
- Give you the opportunity to learn from others in your line of work (find them through search and hash tags; discussed later), and interact within that community.
- Allow you to see who's doing the good stuff in your field, and get ideas to apply to your own.
- Help you build customers by friending like-minded people online.
- Offer an effective, fresh, and friendly way for handling customer service issues.

Twitter: The Answer to a Short Attention Span?

Engaging your community on Twitter can be easier or harder than doing so on other online forums, depending on how you look at it. It's easier in that you don't have to think of a long, drawn-out post, but somewhat more challenging because you have to compact your message into 140 characters or fewer! If you know how to text on your phone, you already have some experience here. Twitter is a lot like texting, except that you don't have to deal with a tiny keyboard and you have 20 fewer characters to work with.

Twitter is one of the best ways to quickly and easily handle the customer issues of today's savvy online users while building a community. First, though, you'll have to figure whether your customers will be on Twitter. If they are the type that spends a lot of time online, there's a good chance they will be joining Twitter, sooner or later. If, however, you have a brick-and-mortar business or a professional practice, there's a chance your customers may not be. Only you can gauge this. While there's always a chance that a new platform might be forthcoming, I'm betting money that Twitter—or some related form of microblogging—will be around for a while.

You can think of Twitter as very much like the telephone party line in the old days. It's a singular line that carries a number of subscribers in one circuit. But they are texting, not talking, and the messages and information can be seen by thousands of people when they are retweeted. That makes it an effective way to gather real-time market intelligence, collect feedback, and build relationships with your customers, partners, and other people who care about your company. It's also an easy way to make new customers.

Part of Twitter's magic is that you can check it at any hour of any day or night to catch up on comments directed to you

(@ replies, or "at" replies). You can search the site for posts that relate to your business and answer them.

The best aspect of microblogging, however, is being able to look at the Twitter stream of people you follow to see what's on their minds. Just because they're not talking to *you* doesn't make what they say any less important or interesting. Become part of the conversation by *reaching out* and responding to those who raise questions you can answer. It's a worthy investment in your ever-growing customer community. Your customers are migrating to these microblogging sites, and when they get there, they'll be glad to see that you are there, too.

Your *tweets*—the term for comments on Twitter—are indexed by Google search. As the search engine optimization experts will tell you, the more often your brand appears on the Web, the faster— and more frequently—you'll get noticed. The more quality content you "push" on Twitter, the sooner your community will grow.

But people will follow you only if your tweets are engaging. This is one area where it's not all about your business. Twitter is transparent, which means people will get to know you *and* your company. You're here to build an online presence for your business, so make your tweets interesting and your content rich (more on content shortly).

It is also important to talk not just about yourself; *conversing* with community is the way to win followers here. Award-winning social, search, and viral marketing scientist and author Dan Zarrella views marketing and social media from an analytical perspective. His posts at danzarella.com look at the online world from a very scientific slant. To determine the best approach to gain followers on Twitter, Dan did an analysis of more than 60,000 accounts using his TweetPsych.com tool, which creates psychological profiles of the public Twitter account and compares it to the thousands already in the database. Dan looked at

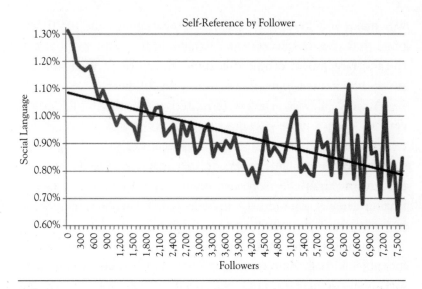

Figure 6.1 Tweeting is all about joining the conversation, not marketing yourself.

accounts whose users speak about themselves—in other words, broadcast messages to their followers. Here's Dan's analysis of the chart resulting from his research, shown in Figure 6.1: "What I found here is pretty clear: Accounts that have more followers do not tend to talk about themselves much. Want more followers? Stop talking about yourself."

More ideas on how to use Twitter coming up in the next section, on content.

Generating Appealing Content

Simply put, you must have interesting content. Luckily, on Twitter, you don't have to write it all yourself; you can tweet links to interesting articles. That said, don't *just* retweet other people's news; unless a story is highly newsworthy, retweeting too often will make you look lazy. Search the Web every day for timely posts that your followers would likely find interesting or helpful; the more recent, the better. Even scanning news Web sites for stories will garner appreciation from your followers.

A recent Pew Research Center report says that a full 75 percent of online news consumers get news stories delivered via e-mail or social networking, and 52 percent of those people will share news stories with others online. It was also found that 72 percent of American news consumers say they follow the news because they enjoy talking with others about what is happening in the world. Again, it all comes down to conversation.

This is your opportunity to share something of value. Search for subjects that relate to your industry or even business in general. News aggregator sites—sites that do the Internet scouring for you and post the links to stories all on one page—can be invaluable resources. Here are a few sites where you might search for timely news items:

- *Alltop.* @GuyKawasaki's Alltop.com is a firehouse of information. You can find articles on almost any subject here. It's easy to locate your referred topic by using the site's built-in search engine.
- *Google News.* If you want to be the first with the latest in news, send your browser to news.google.com. Google aggregates news from newspapers and syndicates. News loads continually on the site, so if you keep the page up while you're working and notice a story that captures your interest, you can get the jump on the world and post the latest content.
- *PopURLs.* This is another site that you can customize to show you only the subjects you're interested in as they pop up in the news. Sign up at popurls.com with almost any openID. The OpenID scheme allows you to sign in to numerous sites

without going through a tedious individual setup. You can use your Google, Yahoo!, Blogger, Flickr, Facebook, or Twitter logins—plus more—for entry, and you'll be tweeting your favorite topics in seconds.

- *Pop Culture News.* If your audience is fascinated by the latest goings-on with celebrities and pop culture icons, check sites like newser.com or tmz.com. These sites present rapid-fire updates, so there's always something new to link to.
- *Bing.* Not to be outdone by Google, Microsoft has bing.com. Click the link for news. From the home page, the flyout from the news link lets you go directly to general, business, entertainment, or local news.

Be sure to use a URL shortener like bit.ly, tinyurl.com, or owl.ly, for brevity.

More Ideas for Using Twitter

- *Add personal thoughts or quotes.* If you can't think of anything pithy at the moment, search the Web for quotes from someone you admire. Mark Twain, Winston Churchill, and Ben Franklin are the obvious ones, so be more creative. Whomever you quote, however, remember to credit the person who made the original statement.

    Lotay Yang, founder of Black Card Circle and the not-for-profit Black Card Circle Foundation, uses Twitter in the best of ways, by promoting both his cause and his brand. Take a look at his stream, @Lotay, in Figure 6.2.

- *Retweet information of value.* Retweeting is vital; passing content from one group of followers to another is the very thing that makes Twitter so interesting. Don't get too carried away with this, however, as it can become annoying to your followers. But if you see a tweet from someone that you find

Figure 6.2 Lotay promotes his community causes, along with offering quotes and conversation.

particularly interesting, use the ReTweet function and duplicate the tweet in your stream. People appreciate it when you share valuable information.

- *Address comments that are directed to you.* As I've emphasized previously, communication is a two-way street; responding is just common courtesy. Moreover, two-way conversations help build your community and add interest to your tweets. Twitter is best when it becomes a conversation.

- *Listen regularly for mention of your business or line of business.* Send helpful @ replies to comments from others of like mind, and follow them. Give suggestions, ideas, and advice. Thank people for praise; conversely, handle graciously any customer complaints that haven't been directed to your account.

- *Search for people looking for deals on items you sell.* Go to http:// search.twitter.com and perform a search on the items you sell. When you see someone asking about where to get the best deal on exactly what it is you offer, tweet back with an exclusive coupon! @DellOutlet does this very successfully every day; in fact, Dell attributes $6.5 million in sales during 2009 to its product-specific promotions on Twitter. Dell has more than 80 accounts on Twitter, all of which are maintained by a Dell staff member or team.

- *Ask questions.* On Twitter, this is called *crowd sourcing*, and it's very effective. It's a great way to engage the community and learn more about topics that interest you or that could help grow your business. Everyone has an opinion, so what better way to find out what your community is thinking or wanting than by asking questions? If, say, you have a restaurant, float an idea about a new menu item or service, and see if someone salutes!

- *Spark a discussion.* Another way to build the one-on-one engagement that you're looking for is to mention a current event or jump on an idea. Your engagement with strangers will help build your community.

- *Check out local trends.* Twitter has a new "trending topics" area that's featured on your home page. Discover what's hot in your city by scrolling down and finding Local Trends in the right-hand column. You can home in on what interests the members of your community, and perhaps get an idea of something to tweet about or comment on.

- *Be relatable.* Never lose sight of the fact that human beings take part in activities other than work. You're not a robot; it's completely acceptable to show a little of your personal side. Twitter is about sharing, so share! Share the fun stuff with your followers. Perhaps a blow-by-blow account of your child's Little League game would be a bit much, but share when you've been to a film, found a new restaurant, or connected in real life with someone you originally met on Twitter. It's the personal tweets that keep your stream interesting.

- *Send out a business message.* Give a discount coupon for your Web site, or post information on a current sale at your store. When a new product arrives, tweet about it! Be careful to limit these self- and company-promoting tweets, however, or your stream will look like spam and no one will choose to follow you.

People use Twitter in many different ways—as many ways as there are to make Bloody Marys (I like mine with a crisp bacon swizzle, thank you). There is truly is no right or wrong. Use these suggestions as guidelines, to help you achieve your goal of building a community and interacting with your customers.

And while you are paying attention to the things you *can* do, here are a few things to be sure *not* to do:

- *Don't ignore your followers.* It's good to follow back real and talkative people who follow you. It shows that you are interested in them.
- *Don't spam.* Do not send unsolicited business @ messages to people you don't know, and don't send automated promotional direct messages (DM) when someone follows you. If you want to thank a new follower, an open @ message or a thank-you in a DM will set a much more positive tone for future conversations.

- *Don't retweet your own messages.* You may have other Twitter accounts, or perhaps other people in your company are tweeting your news. People can clearly see who is related to your company. If they see that you're constantly retweeting someone else, they will click the link to see who it is. On Twitter you won't fool anyone in the long run. Retweeting promotions from a confederate's account is disingenuous and dishonest.
- *Don't continually send tweets from an automated server.* Though it's common practice to send automated tweets, it can seem inauthentic. When a tweet is posted, the platform that sent it is identified. When the tweet appears automatically via an application program interface (API)—using a software program to interface with a platform—to create a false presence, that is visible to those following you. If you are trying to reach customers in a time zone other than yours, it's okay to schedule a tweet or two to reach them. (They'll know you're not up at that hour, anyway.) It's pretty much a waste to tweet deep-thinking, Zen-like quotes then send them out in such an insincere fashion.
- *Don't use Twitter as your business PR stream.* One self-serving tweet after another is not going to make people interested in what you have to say. Many major brands—even those that are supposedly the sources of top customer service—run glaring examples of how *not* to engage, by providing a daily automated broadcast of what they're doing. Yawn.
- *Don't neglect your bio.* You have exactly 160 characters to use keywords that describe you and your business; it's the only way people will know who you really are. Don't waste this valuable real estate. Figure 6.3 clearly shows how Dr. Phil plans to use Twitter to engage his followers.

Figure 6.3   Although informative, Dr. Phil's bio is not exactly an invitation to engage.

Twitter Chats and #hashtags

You will notice when you are on Twitter tweets from people with hash tags (indicated by the number symbol, #) preceding them. The #hashtag also may be followed by strange abbreviations, several words run together, or single topics. Hash tags are used to help spread and organize information on Twitter. They make subjects easier to find and search for. Conferences, major events, and even disasters (e.g., #earthquake) can help put in order specific tweets and make it easier for you find people with similar interests. It's a great way to do research, learn, or to exchange ideas with others.

Hash tags are also used to identify regularly scheduled Twitter chats that are organized live on the site. Twitter thought leaders (perhaps even you?) institute and moderate these weekly chats on many varied topics. I've seen as many as 150 people participating in these chats online. Finding them is a bit easier using Twitter's Summize search, http://search.twitter.com. Using sites such as www.tweetchat.com, www.wthashtag.com, or www.twubs.com make the conversations easier to follow and are simple to use. These sites automatically append each of your tweets with the chat's hash tag. This allows you to filter out all conversation and see just the chat's comments, for easy interaction.

You don't need an invitation to join; feel free to jump in with a comment if you see one of these chats (just be sure to use the appropriate hash tag in your tweet so participants will see your comment).

Here's a (very) short list of some of the hash tags:

- *#AGchat*: People in the business of growing food, fuel, feed, and fiber.
- *#BlogChat*: Experts and newbies in blogging.
- *#CarChat*: Automotive enthusiasts.
- *#CookChat*: A chat for foodies, chefs, and novices in the business of food preparation.
- *#CustServ*: For those in any industry with an interest in customer service.
- *#EyeConnect*: For optometrists, ophthalmologists, and other eye-care professionals.
- *#FollowReader*: Book readers, publishers, authors, librarians, and bloggers.
- *#GardenChat*: Open to all with an interest in gardening.
- *#JournChat*: Conversation between journalists, bloggers, and PR folks.
- *#MDChat*: The world's first Twitter chat for doctors.
- *#PetChat*: Ongoing dialog about pets.
- *#SocPharm*: Pharmaceutical marketing and social media.

I founded the Tuesday night customer service chats on Twitter with Jeffrey Kingman (@JeffreyJKingman), which gathers an interesting group of people from consumers to customer service professionals. Participants often speak about customer service issues they have had and, perhaps, haven't had the time to work out with the company. When customers have been on the phone for over an hour, they aren't happy about spending another hour online to complain. In contrast, when customers voice complaints about a company during our chats, the company often joins in the conversation to solve the issue. But that's not always even necessary, because proper monitoring allows them to address the issues within hours.

Having your own Twitter account and using it to monitor your brand makes sense. Lots of big companies now have Twitter accounts, though most use them for announcements and advertising. That's all well and good, but it's very Web 1.0.

Tweet Frequency

People often ask me, "How often should I tweet?" That's really up to you, and depends upon the amount of time you have to devote to making social connections with your customer. Some days you may have more time than others, so it may be best to keep it organic.

There are those who feel they always have to be "in the game," tweeting continually. Many of these folks use automated services like FutureTweets or HootSuite to post their tweets on a timed basis to make it *seem* like they're online. But what happens if someone responds to your tweet and you're not there? If you're playing in the Twitterworld, you need to check in at least once a day to respond and acknowledge those who have directed messages to you. Conversing, even with time lapses, is key.

When you're building your community, start slow. Begin by tweeting a few times a day; you can always do more over time. In order to engage a community, you're going to have to be posting on the site with regularity. It's an expected give-and-take.

When should you tweet? Just as closing auctions on eBay have their best hours, and television has its "prime time," there are specific time periods on Twitter when your tweets will reach the largest number of people. I've studied this aspect of the Internet for years, to refine auction timing, and then blended my past experience with what I've learned from Twitter.

If you have a brick-and-mortar business, you'll want to send your tweets to accommodate people local to it. If yours is a Web-based business and draws customers from across the United States, your morning window is between 9:00 AM and 1:00 PM Pacific Standard Time (PST) and noon to 4:00 PM Eastern Standard Time (EST). Think about it: On the West Coast, you'll reach individuals just sitting down at their desks or drinking coffee in front of their computers, and through lunch. Your East Coast followers will be in their late afternoon—just before leaving the office. You also get Eastern Europeans at this time, just winding up work for the day. These are the busy Twitter hours, and a good time to take advantage of the morning and evening crowds.

You might also find it interesting to learn that, aside from a few who are always on the site, you'll reach a different crowd in the morning than you will in the evening. So if you have an interesting tweet to share, repeating it with slightly different verbiage 12 hours later is a good strategy. This tactic can also help reach international users.

If you want to get scientific and home directly in on your community, use a URL shortener, as I mentioned earlier. Doing so lets you know the number of clicks you get per tweet. You can summarize this data over a length of time to find the time frame that is most effective for your conversation.

Despite these patterns, keep in mind that tweeting at *any* hour will net you an active and interested audience from all over the world.

To Follow Back or Not?

This is kind of a sticky wicket when it comes to social media sites. There are many big names out in the Twittersphere that do not follow back those who follow them. To answer this question, ask yourself: What do you wish to accomplish online?

- Reach out to as many customers and potential customers as you can.
- Build customer loyalty.
- Listen to what is trending in your area of interest.
- Build a community for your brand.

The best way to do this is to get people to feel invested in what you have to say. Twitter customer service and marketing are far more successful when you listen and respond. Connecting to other human beings equals *listening*.

Building community requires that you *include* people—or at least make them *feel* included. People have a need to be included; simply put, it makes them feel good. There is no caste system in social media; it is a connector of people from varied backgrounds and lifestyles. Making a person feel part of what you're doing goes a long way to making him or her want to cheer you on and find more people to join with you. That's how this whole "social side" of dealing with customers works. You want them to be more than just fans of your business. Including people helps get them invested.

Let's say you're a huge admirer of an author, a technology guru, a movie star, or a recording artist—and that just once he or she answered back to one of your tweets. Better yet? The celebrity followed you back! I've experienced this, and silly as it seems, it felt good. I felt like I was part of the person's community. It's just human nature; we all love to be heard and considered. We all like to believe that our thoughts are of value to others.

DISH Network is a company that believes in following back. In Chapter 13, Lessons from Big Business, I share with you their philosophy.

You can enhance your connection with different groups of people on Twitter by using Twitter lists. You can easily make a private list consisting of your core customers and friends, which cannot be seen by your followers or anyone else. This gives you a clear view of the conversation with your closest connections, without the distraction of thousands of tweets.

Direct Messaging

Following back people on Twitter gives people the opportunity to send you direct messages—DM, in Twitter slang. This means that they can engage you in a private exchange that does not appear on the public stream. If you find that a user you've followed abuses the privilege, you can "unfollow" or "block" that individual with a click of your mouse.

There's a level of responsibility that comes with the privilege of being able to DM someone. Some Twitter members send out an automated DM to new followers. But because there are so many people now using this method, it has lost its appeal to many as a sign of welcome; worse, some people tend to look at these messages as spam.

If you really feel that you must send a welcome DM to everyone who follows you, do something *for* them. Thank them for the follow, and offer a free cookie with their lunch on their next visit, free shipping on an order from your store, or a free dog biscuit for their pet. And don't make them go out of their way to receive the gift from you.

Once you start receiving direct marketing messages from people you follow, you'll be able to tell how authentic they sound. Social customer outreach is about your customers, conversing with them and solving issues—and a *little* promotion. Your sincerity is in your transparency; the online community can see through cheap marketing tactics.

There's no way you will be able to see each and every tweet that your followers post every day; and honestly, no one expects it. When they direct a comment to you (@ reply) it's not likely you can respond each and every time. But it's good practice to attempt to do so as often as you can. Your audience will feel included and your service to your community will be validated.

Reading what the people *you* follow have to say can help you understand shifts in the market before they happen. This isn't a time waster; it's simply smart business and effective customer service.

Here are a few more tips for encouraging a growing follower list and making your Twitter experience successful:

- *Use your name as your Twitter handle.* Doing so will make you easier to find in the Twitter directory.
- *Post a picture.* Before you tweet a single word, put up a head shot of yourself, a flattering photo. Unless you are a huge brand and have a staff tweeting for you, *you* are the face of your brand. People want to see what you look like. (And although they can be cute, please do not put in a photo of your dog.)
- *Fill out the bio.* This is where you are restricted to 160 characters or fewer to talk about yourself and your business. This is

the most valuable real estate on Twitter because what you say here can make or break you with prospective followers. Avoid using self-important words like *expert, rock star,* or *maven.*

- *Search regularly for the name of your business or brand.* People may not know you are active on Twitter and may make a comment in their stream about your business. How cool is it that you find that mention and respond to the person? Very.
- *Do not use the default background for your Twitter home page.* If you're handy with graphics, design a custom background. Examine the backgrounds of pages you like to get an idea of what you want to put on yours. In the meantime, you can get a free background by searching Google for free twitter backgrounds; or go to a site such as www.socialidentities.com. Hugh Briss (@HughBriss), who runs the site, has an excellent eye for what's right. If you are sure you know what you want, he can design a custom background using your photographs and information.
- *Remember to tweet often.* This is the most important tip. People like it when they are part of something bigger—and, hopefully, very soon that will be your home community on Twitter.

Kingly and Queenly Engagement

A king or a queen has to maintain a sense of poise, so I use the image of royalty as an example of how we can best portray ourselves online. Perhaps it comes from the perfect manners our parents hoped we'd have, or perhaps just how we like to see the world. Your online reputation is fragile, so it's critically important to never allow yourself to post without thinking.

There may very well be times while you're interacting with your customers and your community when your first instinct will be to want to fire off a nasty response to someone who is complaining. But, clearly, this won't help you instill loyalty in your customers or develop your following. Never forget, once you put your words out there, they are there to stay, and anything you say might be taken the wrong way, and put a serious dent in your reputation.

Sad to say, the more popular you and your business become online, the more people may want to bash you, take advantage of you, or merely flame you in public. It is guaranteed to happen eventually, so be prepared. People may also make outrageous demands of you and your time. How you respond to these requests will reflect indelibly on your public persona.

Being graceful is a kingly (or queenly) state. You have to be able to rise above your anger and take a step back. Remind yourself that anytime you post on Twitter your words can be indexed by Google, quoted in a thousand blogs, or—one way or another—end up on the home page of the *New York Times*. Once you've posted your comments, people will see them and may use them to make judgments of you.

The rule of thumb is, take a breath before responding; this applies to both social media and in-person interactions. Think of how a king or queen would react to this sort of comment from his or her audience. You need to maintain your poise at all costs, and give a legitimate (and respectful) response.

I gave this advice to *Trust Agents* author Chris Brogan, and subsequently he included his thoughts on it in his January 1 post, "My 3 Words for 2010":

> She [Marsha Collier] said that I should "be kingly" with regards to managing criticism . . . that essentially meant that I needed to maintain poise and balance and charm and demeanor when dealing with life's unpleasant moments. I've

thought of that phrase quite often since, and have evolved it to include my business passions—and so it becomes one of my three guiding words for how I conduct myself and business in 2010.

In the end, your online engagement is what will build success online. Your customers need to be assured they can connect and communicate with you. There's no difference between you and them; we're all in this online world together. Start now with your online engagement, so that it will become second nature to you. You'll find that the time investment you make online will be rewarding.

7

Checking Out Where Customers Review Your Business

There was a time when the general public had to rely on newspapers, magazines, and television for reviews of restaurants, books, and films. And getting references to most service professionals was almost like sharing trade secrets—from friend to friend or colleague to colleague, over the phone and in person. With the invention of the Internet, eBay started a feedback system; and around the same time, "real people" began posting reviews on Amazon. A whole new world for reviewing began.

Business always knew that marketing could bring great results, and word-of-mouth recommendations were considered golden. Now, we only have to visit Web sites to get information and real-world data on just about everything from solar toothbrushes to dentists.

No brand or profession is immune from scrutiny these days, and you need to know where your customers are looking for counsel before they select providers or purchase products. Anyone can get word-of-mouth data from sites that specialize in almost every profession, product, company, or store. You may be surprised to learn that there are more than 30 sites that compile opinions on medical professionals alone—the leaders being Angie's List, RateMDs.com, HealthGrades.com, Vitals.com, and Vimo.com.

Although the niche, specialized sites are popular, it seems that the most consumer reviews are posted on generalized sites. The venerable Better Business Bureau already had its own Web site but soon saw the importance of community comments and started another site for "real people" reviews, Trustlink.org. It may be big, but Web citizens have their own favorite sites, several of which I describe here.

Yelp.com

Although this site began by covering only restaurants, Yelp.com has expanded to cover all sorts of retail businesses in its local consumer-generated reviews. People regularly go to the site for person-to-person recommendations on businesses of all kinds. In August 2010, Yelp quoted a reach of 38 million visitors per month, and 12 million local reviews (over 85 percent rate a business with three stars or higher).

Yelp.com currently offers business reviews in most major cities in the United States, and is expanding rapidly—first in the United Kingdom. When you visit Yelp for the first time, you may be surprised to see that your business is probably already on the site, because Yelp gets its listings from many sources and puts companies up for discussion.

When someone chooses to review your business listing, he or she can leave a commentary-style review and post a rating of one to five stars. The rating appears at the top of the page and reflects an average of the rating you've received from each person's review.

Yelp can help your business in several ways. It allows you to build exposure for your company, monitor public opinion of how you're doing, and facilitate research as to what your local community wants from an organization like yours.

All you need is about an hour to set up your page.

Yelp offers a free set of tools that you can access by going to yelp.com/business to set up your free business account. The basic account gives you the opportunity to track the number of people who view your page, post offers and photos, and communicate with the customers who post. An enhanced toolset is available for businesses with multiple locations, for about $75 a month. The site also sends out a weekly e-mail newsletter to its users as a local edition.

Once you've got your business page set up, the posts you provide—announcements, valuable discounts, or in-store events—may just land you your own personal space in the Yelp newsletter. There's also the chance that your discounts may pop up on other local profile pages, as in the AJ Bombers listing shown in Figure 7.1. The benefits for signing up are clear:

- *Communicate with your customers.* Yelp gives you the opportunity to answer your customers on your business's public page, for all to see—or, if you prefer, you can answer comments privately. Since engaging customers is what the online world is all about, a personal message to each reviewer will go a long way toward building your transparency and loyalty.
- *Set up a profile page as you might in any social network.* Take note, however, that this one is all about your business, and requires

Figure 7.1 AJ Bombers reviews are so positive that they may outweigh any competitors' ads.

you to include all pertinent information. Yelp's administration page for your company owners gives you a ton of choices for sharing your business information with your customers. Be precise and honest, so that prospective customers will know exactly what to expect when they walk in your door, whether brick-and-mortar or digital. Be sure to mention anything and everything that makes your business special—any information that might convert a Web site browser to a regular, paying customer. Fill out as much as possible, and be sure to keep it up to date.

- *Track how many people view your business profile.* Do this by regularly checking the bar graph on your admin page.
- *Add extras to your profile.* These might include photos, a detailed business description, updated information, a company history, or a list of your specialties.
- *Receive review alerts.* When your business page is updated with a new post, Yelp will send you an e-mail alert so you don't have to check your page every day.
- *Offer special discounts to Yelp users.* Be sure that these are valuable enough to cause a customer who's on the edge to make the decision to come to your business. Direct these discounts specifically at Yelp users.
- *Announce upcoming events.* Yelp gives you 140 characters to announce a company-sponsored event. Use your marketing skills here to craft an appealing title. Make your statement read like a tabloid newspaper headline, and be sure to include a shortened URL to link to a page where users can access further information.

Should your business offer a Wi-Fi connection to your customers, it's a smart idea to place a table-tent card for your customers that mentions your Yelp business URL, along with your other social network affiliations.

Angie's List

If you don't already know about AngiesList.com, you should—especially if you have a service business. Angie's List is a subscription-only regional aggregator of consumer reviews of local service providers that bases subscription prices on where you live.

These days, as customers influence one another more than companies do, Angie's List recognizes this trend by providing an

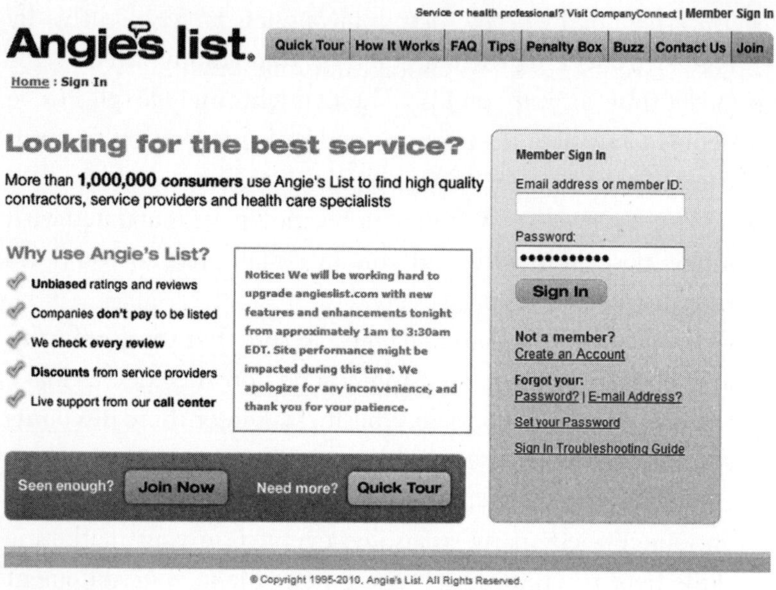

Figure 7.2 On its home page, Angie's List establishes itself as the destination for service reviews.

open forum for people to recommend, or warn other users about plumbers, roofers, gardeners, handymen, and more. The site claims over a million consumer members, and reports receiving approximately 40,000 new consumer reviews on service companies each month. The site does not allow the posting of anonymous reviews, as it expects its members to "take responsibility for their words."

Reviews are a bit more structured on Angie's List than they are on Yelp, as it uses a standard format that consumers must follow. Angie's List also averages the reports to give them a letter grade, A through F.

Your business can receive reviews on Angie's List whether or not you register at the site. However, registering allows you to:

- Read and respond to the reviews.
- Update your company's contact information.
- Upload photos of your current work.

To register your business at the site, visit https://company .angieslist.com.

Angie's List has recently added medical professionals, photographers, and interior designers—just about every service you use in your everyday life. So if you have a service business, this is definitely a site you should monitor. It also has a Company Connect department, which can help you respond to reviewers, and acts as a liaison between customers and contractors. If your business receives a complaint on the site, you might be put in the "Penalty Box," for all consumers in your area to see if you don't respond.

Other Sites to Watch

There are some other sites to keep an eye on, in case they expand to include user-generated reviews:

- *Citysearch* was a pioneer on the Web in 1995. It began more as a listing service, and reviews are mostly staff written. It is now one of the leading online local guides that enables consumers to stay connected, offering access to neighborhood restaurants, bars, shopping, and beauty and professional services across every zip code in the United States.
- *Insider Pages* is the local user-generated branch site from CitySearch. Launched in 2004, Insider Pages was created to help people find the best local businesses through recommendations from "their friends and neighbors." These pages cover most trades and professions, and import medical reviews from medicalgrades.com.

- *MerchantCircle*, started in 2005, is more of a community for small businesses, though it claims more than 5 million monthly views for its sites in over 50 states. I found a minimal number of customer reviews on the site, but it is growing as a local source.

Handling Reviews

If you receive a bad review from an online community member, you can deal with the issue immediately and turn the customer around quickly with your brilliantly executed customer service. Once you've solved the problem, your new raving fan can update his or her initial review and tell the world how great you are.

The same rule applies here as to responding to a negative comment on your Web site: Do not to go off half-cocked when you come across a less-than-glowing review of your business. Take a deep breath and reign in your emotions first. Sit down quietly and read the review closely. You may find some honesty there—albeit off-putting—that you hadn't previously considered. You may even find a distinct flaw in the way you do business; and while that certainly doesn't feel good, it *will* help you solve problems in the future.

Next, investigate the issue with your staff, and once you've gotten over the initial insult, contact the reviewer and offer to make things right. When he or she sees you've been working toward a resolution, that negative attitude may take a 180-degree turn.

You may find that the customer didn't like you or your staff or your service, and that he or she cannot be placated under any circumstances. In such a case, remember there are some things over which you have no control—you can't make everyone a fan. The best you can do is to connect with the customer and show that you care. Once the individual sees that you are interested in his or her opinion—and you offer something to bring him or her back—you may well witness a negative patron turn into the most loyal customer of all. This sort of customer is also one who will probably become your most vocal defender and promoter.

Just keep doing the good work. You can't turn around every person, so simply keep doing your best. It's all you can do.

Conducting business these days is no longer a matter of "if you build it, they will come." Now, engaging your customer is a matter of build it, work it, and be part of it. The saving grace of the hard work you put into the community is that you will enjoy your customers. The more you see them as real people with families and problems like yours, the more you will take pleasure in making them happy online.

The places to build and serve a community will no doubt skyrocket over the next few years. Keep an eye on Twitter for news flashes on new sites, or check my blog and Posterous, where I'll be updating this information regularly.

8

Knowing Your Customers' Expectations

How to Connect

Today, as never before, online media enable businesses everywhere to reach customers across a massive geographic area. Given how wide that area is, how do you find out about the people you want to connect with? You've heard of advertising being targeted to the "lucrative" socioeconomic-segmented demographic (by age, education, and income), but what about all the other groups? Who are they, and how will you recognize them? Figuring out what drives your customers will allow you to better communicate with them. Keep in mind that when you're in business, you shouldn't consider yourself as only a vendor with customer service issues to deal with; you have to be a marketer, too.

You need to determine who buys what you sell. Better put, you must decide which types of customers you want to interact with. There are, for example, different customer service issues for a company selling skateboards than one selling video games or fashion; they represent clearly different market segments and different people. When expanding your product lines or customer base, consider that you may not wish to deal with the snarky comments that might come from certain groups.

By studying what makes the various generations tick, you can spread your business out into areas that best suit your own personality and business style. It's that style that will make your online customer service outreach successful. Feeling uncomfortable dealing with a specific audience will, in the long run, make you unhappy. (At the end of this chapter I'll share a story about how big brands missed an opportunity with a huge market because they didn't understand the customers in it.)

There are plenty of blanket definitions out there meant to describe the general population based on its members' stages in life: what they are "expected" to buy, and the activities they participate in. Though your experience as an entrepreneur may shoot holes in these generally accepted theories, everything must have a "standard," and the generational standards define demographic groups and classify them by age and the mores of their contemporaries.

Although the U.S. Census Bureau delineates generations, the true demographics of generations are not formed solidly by biological birth dates. You can go to five different references and find five different ideas of how the dates skew. Individuals react more based on their life experiences and the events that influenced them as they grew up. News stories, economic shifts, and other memorable cultural incidents all play a role in how each group's emotional characteristics developed. We know that outside influences make a major difference in how each of us perceives our world, which affects how and why we buy things and the way in which we relate to different messages.

If your friendship circle and/or customer base trends over varying age groups, you've no doubt heard comments like, "Why don't they ever answer the phone?" "What's with this texting thing?" "Why can't I ever speak to a live person?"

There is an interesting piece of data that throws a monkey wrench into traditional theories about demographics, however: The number of 18- to 34-year-olds living at home with their parents increased from 8.3 million in 1960 to 19.2 million in 2007, according to the nonprofit Network on Transitions to Adulthood. Calling this group "boomerangers," a 2009 Pew Research study exposed further game-changing data:

- 13 percent of parents with adult children say at least one has moved back home in the past year.
- 10 percent of adults ages 18 to 34 blame the economy for their move back home.
- 11 percent of all adults 18 or older live with their parents.
- 7 in 10 adult children who live with their parents are under 30 (30 percent over 30!).
- Of adults reporting they live with their parents, 35 percent say they lived alone prior to returning home.

This represents a huge shift in traditional generational placement. In the 1950s and 1960s, adult children got married at a younger age, perhaps lived with parents or in-laws for a year, and saved money to buy a home. In 1960, the U.S. Census Bureau reported that about 6.3 million adults aged 18 to 24 lived at home; that number more than doubled, to 15 million, in the 2008 estimates. This means that purchasing decisions, buying patterns, and possibly many other behaviors have dramatically changed for this age group.

Prior to the economic downturn, children completing their schooling were expected to get a job and move out of the family home. Today, the traditional college fund has to stretch further than in the past; the under-30 group needs help surviving financially. The 2007 study also established that an astounding 75 percent of 18- to 24-year-olds receive money from their parents; for 40 percent of those young people, it amounts to at least $10,000 a year.

Statistics like these can certainly make it difficult to determine exactly where customer money is coming from and exactly *who* your customer is, because those Baby Boomer parents influence which items their adult children purchase more so than they did in the past. It's the "other" golden rule: "He who has the gold, makes the rules." That makes part of the challenge for small businesspeople to find a way to please bigenerational customer households.

Luckily, the rate of adoption of online social media is about equal when one compares the Boomer category to the under-30 demographic. Flying (again) in the face of traditional thinking, the fastest-growing group of Facebook users is women age 55 and older, up 175 percent since September 2008. A Cable & Telecommunications Association for Marketing (CTAM) Pulse report showed that 77 percent of online Americans ages 65 and older say they shop online, representing the highest percentage among all generational groups.

This reflects a direct transition from face-to-face interaction to the online media world. Translation? Reaching people online is more social and less confrontational, and addressing your customer's needs can be perceived as community building for your brand or business.

Defining the Generations

The "generation gap"—as it was once called—is narrowing. Although the age differences are clear, the wants and needs of the different age groups are often quite similar. Adding chaos to the generational discussion is the fact that there are no universally specific age ranges or dates for the generations—there are as many variables involved in naming them as there are statisticians who try to do it. For the ease of this discussion, I've broken the groups into very general categories here, based on life experiences.

World War II Generation

Sometimes called the Silent Generation (coined by *Time* magazine in a 1951 cover story, when they were coming of age), or the "Matures," this group comprises a comparatively small number, based on the low birthrates during the economic crisis of the time—an estimated 52 million people. This segment of our population was born from 1925 to 1945. The eldest of this demographic have lived through the Great Depression and know firsthand what sacrifice is about. A few from this age group ran for the office of the president, but didn't win: Ron Paul, John McCain, Michael Dukakis, John Kerry, and the Reverend Jesse Jackson.

They don't like waste, purchase items in smaller quantities, and prefer using single-serving products. World War II colored their lives in many ways, not the least of which was to encourage them to work together against a common enemy. This generation also is generally more team-oriented than other age groups, and tends to have plenty of money to spend.

If you work in fund-raising, for example, the World War II generation would be your target customers. According to a recent study by nonprofit software company Convio, these individuals are leaders in cause donations; a whopping 79 percent gives to charitable causes (Boomers are second, at 67 percent).

This generation is a wide-open market; it has many needs and wants. Just look at the success of businesses that sell glasses for the visually impaired, anti-ageing products or health-related items like vitamins, prescription medications, and home medical equipment. The growth of the Internet has also prompted many of these people to have fun unloading their lifelong collections of "stuff" on eBay. And surprising to many, their online usage rivals that of younger generations. According to a study by CTAM:

> Seniors aged 65 and older (also referred to as "Matures") have made the Internet an integral part of their everyday lives. In fact, when it comes to shopping online, Matures lead all other generational groups when it comes to this online activity. They regularly use e-mail (94 percent), go to the Internet to look up health and medical information (71 percent), read news (70 percent), and manage their finances and banking (59 percent). Matures also turn to the Internet for gaming; approximately half (47 percent) of online Matures regularly play free online games.

Matures feel they have accomplished a lot in their lives and have learned life's lessons. Therefore, your online customer service for this group needs to appeal to their sense of independence, rather than treating them as helpless. Give them bonuses for dealing with your business; loyalty programs are strong with this group.

Having grown up with newspapers, they are a coupon-cutting group; today, they appreciate coupons they can print and cut out. So offer discounts to make up for, say, an error made by your company. Because of the economy they've been forced to alter their spending plans and appreciate that you respect that—and them.

Matures also respond very well to direct mail, patriotism, and traditional family values. They prefer to speak to someone in person when it comes to addressing customer service issues. Your online reach thus needs to include options for ways they can contact you. They expect your respect in all dealings. Personal attention and communication are critical when dealing with members of this generation.

Postwar Generation

This demographic group overlaps with the previous one, loosely estimated as being born between 1942 and 1954. They represent the tail end of the World War II, pre-Boomer generation as they intersect with the accepted Generation of Matures and the Baby Boomers. Most industries underestimate this group's customer potential; only organizations like the American Association for Retired Persons (AARP) acknowledge it. If you think this age group is fading away, just visit the AARP Web site, at www.aarp .org. Studying this site and using a little intuition will give you a very clear picture of what this demographic is interested in. The site suggests a wide swath of merchandise they wish to buy.

The postwar generation has lived through such significant global events as the Korean War, the Civil Rights movement, and the Cold War. They moved to the suburbs with their parents, and were present at the birth of rock 'n' roll. Many now are grandparents, which opens an entirely new area of potential purchases, since many are probably spending quite a bit of time shopping for (and taking care of) little ones. Customer service professionals know this, and you too should keep this in mind when addressing grandparents buying for their grandchildren.

It is with this group that the changeover begins, when social media begins to creep into communications. Though they are open to technology, the postwar generation may still prefer personal contact over the phone or via e-mail.

Baby Boomers and Leading-Edge Boomers

This is the second-largest segment of the U.S. population, so it's high time that we concentrated on discovering how they're really spending their time and money. Born between 1945 and 1964, their numbers are staggeringly high, representing 78 million

Americans. Most are still working 12-hour days, interested in fitness and nutrition—running both marathons and businesses—and having lots of fun buying all the latest techie toys.

These folks comprise a significant portion of the population that came of age during the last surge of national culture. They've been working and earning money for many years and now are ready to spend it. They witnessed events like the first man walking on the moon and so grew up thinking anything was possible; at the same time, many other events—such as the Vietnam War, Cuban Missile Crisis, and the assassinations of John F. Kennedy and Martin Luther King Jr.—dulled the optimism of their youth.

It would be a big mistake to ignore the Boomers, for they are both wealthy and tech-savvy enough to want the latest and greatest devices. If you're selling health and wellness products, for example, remember that they love self-improvement products. They've got disposable savings to spend on technology, fashion, restaurants, and travel. (Talk about the market for cosmetics and potions to stave off aging!)

You'll want to take a more "subcultural" tone when dealing with these customers, as this generation was the first to begin thinking with systematic opposition to their parents, as well as where the online community first took hold. They love participating in chats; they comment on blogs; and they prefer to play an active part in your business.

Trailing-Edge Boomers (Generation Jones or Golden Boomers)

This is another overlap group, born between 1956 and 1964 when Boomer birthrates began to decline. Culturally, this group is not the widely promoted Boomers, but not quite Gen Xers, either.

President Barack Obama is a member of this group; he is a Boomer by birth, though considered by many to be a post-Boomer.

Even though they are technically (as defined by the U.S. Census Bureau) the same generation as the Baby Boomers, Trailing-edge Boomers' life experiences make them feel separate from this group. They don't really care about Elvis, didn't want to be hippies, and didn't serve in Vietnam. Among them are the first wave of Reagan-era MBAs who've had their children and are busily starting to spend on them. They're more cynical, too, as they occasionally feel cheated by the large numbers of core-market Baby Boomers (who, in their opinion, got all the good jobs). They view themselves as the "best" generation.

Trailing-edge Boomers entered their adulthood with pessimism; they were the first to enter the workforce with a lack of confidence. Given the heightened expectations of those growing up in the 1960s, they were faced with the realities of the 1970s as they came of age in a far different economic picture. They also are more likely to look for ways to work from home—they're active telecommuters. Considering this attribute, think of all the things you can do to enhance their lives! Embracing the online world, this group treats time as precious, and gives a priority to the concise. With no patience for dilly-dallying, they want to get information on your business quickly and succinctly. They are the target for your FAQs pages and review applications. Court them through e-mail to join your online customer service social media outreach programs.

Trailing-edge Boomers are at the cutting edge of social media users—perhaps not nonstop participants, but more "drive-by" visitors who catch the information online quickly and absorb what they need just as fast. They are the first to look to social media for information on businesses and products, and have a loud public voice when slighted in service. They find it disingenuous to fan or friend a business unless they are really passionate about it.

This group can also tend to be more cynical and less optimistic than the other groups. They view events and service in a pragmatic style, as in "getting what they pay for," and are the first to accept mediocrity in customer service when dealing with discounters. They seem almost to expect to be taken advantage of or disregarded by vendors, so it often takes significant effort to win them over. This is a group with which you must use your "wow" factor, to differentiate your customer service and draw them in.

Generation X

Generation X is another difficult-to-pin-down demographic. The phrase "Generation X" was coined by Douglas Coupland in his 1991 novel, *Generation X: Tales for an Accelerated Culture* (St. Martin's Griffin). (It was also the name of a 1970's musical group featuring famed singer Billy Idol.) Though the term caught on, many retailers and business professionals are still unsure as to whom Generation X refers exactly. It's a hotly debated issue. Some say the Xers were born as early as 1961, others insist as late as 1981; a more accepted time frame places them between 1965 and 1979, when birthrates were at a new low.

Generation Xers were brought up on television and personal computers. They saw the adults around them behaving in incredibly selfish ways, which is something they do not want to repeat in their own lives. They are the first generation to consciously accept safe sex practices and face the possibility of contracting AIDS. They grew up in the "me" generation and now see that the world their parents spoke of was not all that it was cracked up to be, given such scandals as Watergate.

This generation is very concerned with financial and emotional security, which makes them aggressive entrepreneurs— especially given their substantial street-smarts. They think of themselves as being "different," and carry a generational chip on their shoulder; they also want to drop the pretenses of the Baby Boomer–dominated world. Statistically, they are the highest educated age group, as defined by the U.S. Census Bureau. They've had enough of being pummeled by the culture of the Boomers (the Beatles, free love, and the sex lives of their parents) and are desperately trying to carve out their own niche. They're not happy to be the "middle child," sandwiched between the Boomers and the huge numbers of celebrity-loving Millennials. You can appeal to them best through dry humor, coupled with a technical approach. Gen Xers are the perfect target for all kinds of online relationships.

Assume they've already checked your Web site and exhausted all the resources you've supplied to solve their customer service problem. If they have to call you, they're at the last inch of their rope. They want to swiftly find the information themselves. When your customer service representatives speak to Boomers, they need to lightly hand-hold (without being condescending); when speaking with Xers, in contrast, being pleasant is not as important as answering their questions quickly.

Gen Mix

There's an unofficial demographic, born between 1976 and 1985, newly defined by the 2010 "Gen Mix Report," commissioned by VH1, ostensibly to define its core audience. According to the report, Gen Mixers are the group that straddles the line between Gen X and Y: too old to be lumped with Millennials and too young to count as Gen Xers. With all the confusion regarding the dates that mark the beginning of Y and the end of X, it was wide open to someone coming up with a new cohort. The VH1 study, though not exactly recognized as definitive, did determine a couple of interesting points. Gen Mix, the report said, acquires "their sense of optimism and self-confidence from Millennials, and their strong sense of self and security from Gen Xers. They are in a unique life stage and have a unique mind-set. And they're defining adulthood in their own way—proud of their achievements and hopeful for where they're going."

Tom Calderone, president of VH1, said that the report results also revealed that, as a group, viewers of the network "want to connect even more with our characters, our artists, and our celebrities—but in a more genuine way. They still enjoy VH1's signature sense of fun and irreverence, but they also want more storylines that reflect the issues and challenges they are experiencing in their own lives."

In light of this new-age research, Jeff Olde, executive vice president, Original Programming and Production at VH1, says, "We're taking our signature storytelling strengths and amplifying them through three distinct areas: music, celebrities, and real-life stories."

Applying the results of the VH1 study to your online customer service says that you need to appeal to this group's sense of entertainment. Doing business with your company must, therefore, be engaging and current, and empower them to connect. Interaction to them is just as important as reasonable product pricing.

Generation Y

Also known as the Millennials or Generation Next, this group is the largest consumer market since the Baby Boomers. They are the approximately 80 million individuals born between 1977 and 1995—extending to, possibly, the early 2000s—who grew up with the Internet. Although a generation is generally considered to span 20 years, some demographers suggest the actual dates for

Gen Y are 1975 to 2000, whereas others suggest a time frame of 1985 to 2005. *Advertising Age*, the influential magazine for advertising, marketing, and media professionals, coined the term "Gen Y" in 1993, targeting late Xers born between 1974 and 1980, so these are truly children of the advertising era. Having been raised in the 1990s, their parents worked extra hard to strike a balance between work and family, in contrast to the workaholic atmosphere of the 1980s.

Generation Y comprises the children of the Boomers, so they are sometimes called "Echo Boomers," since their large numbers are due to the fact that their huge parental cohort chose to reproduce at this time. Totaling an estimated 80 million members, as noted previously, this generation has finally eclipsed the last birth explosion of 78.2 million Baby Boomers.

Members of Generation Y have been influenced by their parents to value education. They've worked several part-time jobs, and most already know what they want from their careers once they reach the marketplace. To Gen Yers, technology is a fait accompli. They're aware of every up-and-coming trend and are the first to embrace or reject them. The spontaneity of the Internet keeps them ahead of most businesses; for instance, they seem to know what their favorite stars will be wearing almost before the designers and retailers do.

To this cohort, online customer service is crucial to their decision making, as they have the experience to research one company over another; consequently, benefits such as expedited shipping and generous return policies rank high with them. They're style-conscious, tech-savvy, and "prematurely affluent" due to their Boomer parents' prosperity. Millennials appreciate when entertainment is part of the message they receive from retailers. Retro themes are very popular with this group, too, even those reflecting periods as recent as the 1980s.

According to eMarketer, more than 82 percent of U.S. Internet users ages 18 to 34 use social networks at least monthly (and that percentage is likely near 100 percent in target markets). And about 84 percent of Millennials say they don't notice ads on social sites, according to the Lubin School of Business. Reaching out to them through the community, without blatant marketing, is an excellent connection strategy.

Online marketing expert Kelly Mooney, in a 2006 study, found that while Gen Yers are

> self-expressive, confident, and optimistic, they are also assim-ilative, risk averse, and rarely make a purchase decision with-out consulting their peer networks. Just like Boomers, they have strong opinions; but more so than Boomers, they feel compelled to share their opinions with their massive peer networks.

Authenticity and transparency in the way you do business are important to this group. Their interpretation of how things should be done gives them the innate talent to sniff out sleazy sales techniques. So give them a community where they can share with their peers, rather than marketing *at* them.

According to Ken Gronbach, author of *The Age Curve: How to Profit from the Coming Demographic Storm* (AMACOM, 2008), "Gen Y is already consuming at 500 percent of the level of their Boomer parents age for age in adjusted dollars." In other words, this generation may just become the largest spenders in history.

However, the issue of entitlement rears its ugly head with this group. They are sometimes referred to as the "Trophy Generation," a reflection of a current trend in children's com-petitive sports—as well as in many other aspects of their lives—where "no one loses" and everyone gets a trophy, to promote the sense that they've all done well. Many in this cohort are the aforementioned "boomerang" generation, who delay the transition of transitioning into adulthood by living at home.

Members of this generation tend to want lots of attention, and need to feel "special." If you approach this crowd with "what you can do for them," and offer a community with spontaneity, you'll get their attention.

Generation Z

Though some sources pinpoint this generation's emergence to as early as the mid-1980s, the general consensus puts it at the first years of the 2000s. This group grew up without giving technology a second thought; it was second-nature for most of them. They're naturally adept and have been comfortable with technology ever since they were old enough to press the buttons on a keyboard.

Dubbed "Generation Net," this group is almost too young to have established itself in the marketplace, but it will be a driving force in the coming decades. Members of Generation Z come from widely diverse ethnic groups and seem to be more social-cause–oriented than their predecessors. The 2000 Census counted the total population of under 19-year-olds as 80,473,265—28.6 percent of the population. Only time will tell how to most effectively reach this electronically tethered generation of the twenty-first century.

Reaching the Generations with Social Media

Based on the preceding descriptions, you can see how traditional demographic information can help you home in on your customers' needs and desires. The data is also relevant in terms of the social media sites you use in your customer service outreach. In short, you need to be wherever your customers are as they transition online. Savvy social networking methods and customer service can bring new customers to your door and to your Web site.

There are some shocking statistics to consider as you build your community and your online outreach in terms of social networking. Before going into that, though, it's important to point out that almost *all* age groups are online today, in one form or another. Of particular note: Social networks aren't dominated by the youngest (considered the most tech-savvy) generations, but rather by the younger end of what is commonly referred to as "middle-aged" people.

According to a study by Anderson Analytics (provided to and analyzed by eMarketer.com), 13- to 14-year-old members of Generation Z who use social networks were more likely to use MySpace than Facebook, and only 9 percent of them used Twitter. Of those in the study, none used LinkedIn, most likely because they are not looking for jobs as yet. Compare them to Generation Y in Table 8.1. It's interesting to see that three-quarters of that group participated on MySpace, 65 percent on Facebook, 14 percent on Twitter, and 9 percent on LinkedIn. The LinkedIn numbers are significant, since the oldest members of this group are perhaps 30, and the youngest are going into college. These facts beg the questions: Are Gen Yers not interested in getting jobs? Or have they just decided that "fun-employment" (while living with their parents) is a preferred lifestyle? However, it makes sense that Generation X, Baby Boomers, and the World War II generation connect on LinkedIn. The members of these groups have a history of working and are still looking to do so, either salaried or consulting.

How significant is the fact that 9 in 10 older social network users—members of the World War II generation—are on Facebook? As a matter of fact, Facebook usage ranks highest

Table 8.1   Social Networking Sites Used by U.S. Social Network Users, by Generation, May 2009 (percent of respondents in each group)

	Facebook (%)	MySpace (%)	Twitter (%)	LinkedIn (%)
Generation Z	61	65	9	0
Generation Y	65	75	14	9
Generation X	76	57	18	13
Baby Boomers	73	40	13	13
World War II Generation	90	23	17	4

Note: n = 1,000; read chart as saying, 90 percent of social network users from the World War II generation use Facebook.
Source: Anderson Analytics, "Social Network Service (SNS) A&U Profiler," provided to eMarketer, July 13, 2009.

among *all* age groups. This might indicate that the need for community is universal and, possibly, becomes even more important as we grow older. Thus, having an online community presence for your business in order to meet customers' needs is crucial.

It became clear when eMarketer.com analyzed the Anderson Analytics study that the reasons why people join social networks were similar from one generation to the next (see Table 8.2). The report authors wrote that, "Due to the difference in age of the users, [their] interests are naturally different. LinkedIn users are more interested in luxury activities, Twitter users are more interested in pop culture, and MySpace users are more interested in humor/comedy and video games."

What exactly does this mean for customer service? Well, we can conclude from the stats in the two tables that the social influence on the networking sites is defined and easy to target. No matter their age, people visit these sites to meet friends and have fun.

Table 8.2   Reasons that U.S. Social Network Users Joined a Social Network, by Generation, May 2009 (percent of respondents in each group)

	Gen Z (%)	Gen Y (%)	Gen X (%)	Baby Boomers (%)	World War II Gen (%)	Total (%)
Keeping in touch with friends	93	82	71	62	57	75
For fun	91	61	51	38	30	55
Keeping in touch with family	27	40	40	47	51	41
Was invited to use site by someone I know	22	22	30	46	60	30
Keeping in touch with classmates	39	40	27	12	10	30
Keeping in touch with business network	—	3	6	12	2	5
Job searching	—	3	4	10	1	4
Business development/ sales	—	1	6	4	4	3
Recruiting/ searching for information on new hires	—	1	1	0	0	1
Other	6	3	5	3	5	4

Note: n = 1,000

Source: Anderson Analytics, "Social Network Service (SNS) A&U Profiler," provided to www.eMarketer.com, July 13, 2009.

Statistics provide a clearer picture of a given audience or group. The tools that provide this information—like Google AdPlanner (a very handy and free tool for analyzing the demographics of your online community)—are worth studying. Consider the analytics for February 2010: What is the average age of a Twitter or Facebook user? What about the other social networking sites, like MySpace and LinkedIn? To better understand the online world, it's vital to learn how the different ages are distributed among the millions of social network denizens on the Internet.

Google AdPlanner can also be used to determine the traffic (based on cookie estimates), gender, education, and household income at any of these major sites. It's a tremendously helpful resource for advertisers or community advice. Table 8.3 gives some figures.

These statistics reveal that as more generations become comfortable with having technology at their fingertips, they will be spending more time online and, specifically, on social sites. It is, therefore, critical for companies nowadays to keep up with the demographics. You'll want to be sure that if you are looking to

Table 8.3 Age Distribution on Major Social Network Sites

Age Group	0–17 (%)	18–24 (%)	25–34 (%)	35–44 (%)	45–54 (%)	55–64 (%)	65+ (%)
Facebook	7	13	25	20	24	8	2
Twitter	4	13	30	27	17	7	2
Angie's List	1	2	18	28	28	19	4
Yelp	2	6	29	29	21	10	2
Foursquare	1	9	40	32	12	4	1
MySpace	14	18	27	18	17	4	1
LinkedIn	1	4	24	31	26	12	2

Data Source: Google Ad Planner, October 2010.

connect with customers through social networks that you are spending time reaching the right age groups in the right places for your products.

Misunderstanding a Market: A Cautionary Tale

Although this chapter is mainly about understanding your customer, I'd like to end it by sharing with you an example of a "market that got away"—for almost 20 years. By observing changes in social media, and taking the time to reach out to your customers through online customer service, hopefully, something like this would not occur today.

Assuming that we know our customers' needs and desires without checking with them first can result in a huge gap opening between what they want and what we offer them. The old saying that you never know someone until you walk a mile in that person's shoes holds very true both online and off in the twenty-first century. About the only thing you can be sure of these days is that customers want and expect respect and courtesy from the people they do business with.

No matter how well established your business is, you must remember that new audiences are out there. Don't ever miss a marketing opportunity because you are not familiar with a group of people who might need your product or service, or because their interests are different from your own. Your perception of their needs and wants can be quite different from their reality.

Lack of customer respect has resulted in lost customers for many businesses. One of the most egregious marketing faux pas occurred in the first half of the twentieth century. I like to call it "NASCAR blindness."

In the early 1980s, I was general manager of the Los Angeles Dodgers newspaper, *Dodger Blue*. Back then, there were very few women involved in the business of sports. Not that there weren't plenty of female sports fans; there were. But the companies that advertised in the paper were pretty much ignoring the female sports fan market. Today, approximately 60 percent of women follow one sport or another.

In those days, I had a toddler at home and didn't have the time to devote to attending daily baseball games, so I left my job and started my retail marketing company. But I kept my hand in the sports world by founding the publication, *Southern California Auto Racing*. I produced the tabloid more out of love of the sport than business sense. I had to meet the crush of my daily deadlines, and autosports was a pleasing distraction.

The best part of running an autosports publication in Southern California was that there were only five races a year, so I published the tabloid quarterly; it covered NASCAR, open wheel (Indy car), and NHRA drag racing. As much of a community as baseball has, auto racing at the time was even more tightly knit.

My publication was profitable, thanks to national advertisers— profitable enough to enable me to cover races all over the country. The fans were rabid, and the NASCAR family (literally owned by the France family) of fans, teams, and writers were a tightly knit group. It was a great time spent with great people.

I knew a solid market of thousands of people when I saw one. Huge numbers of people went to races with their entire families, and spent a lot of money at them. It was interesting, though, that associated advertising and sponsorships were covered by only a handful of very well-heeled automotive product companies.

PepsiCo was the first to invest, giving Bill France the money he needed to complete construction at Daytona Speedway. (For 50 years, Pepsi-Cola, not Coca-Cola, was served exclusively at Daytona.) In 2008, PepsiCo changed focus, to cosponsor a racing team.

The 1959 Daytona 500 drew a crowd of approximately 42,000 race fans. "Approximately" is a word always applied to auto racing numbers, because the number of tickets sold rarely reflects how many people are in attendance. The infield numbers couldn't possibly be counted, as motor home spots were sold in lieu of single tickets for years. Also, as Bill France once said, "We don't use turnstiles."

Attendance at the Daytona 500 more than doubled by 1964, and by 1975 an estimated 125,000 people watched the great American race. Attendance continued to grow, until at the forty-ninth annual race, in 2007, the event sold out 168,000 seats, with an estimated 80,000 in the infield.

You'd think that attendance figures like this would be enough to attract high-powered sponsors, wouldn't you?

In the early 1970s, sponsorship originally came from leading automotive brands like STP, Purolator, Goodyear, Pennzoil, and the like. Around the same time, a few "out of the box" thinkers jumped aboard, including Anheuser-Busch, R.J. Reynolds Tobacco, Coca-Cola, and Johnson Wax—smart companies. Smart companies that knew they could build their brands and that this was an audience they could sell their products to. In 1979, "renegade" products like Hawaiian Tropic joined in.

Interestingly, NASCAR's peak did not come until well into the late 1990s, when it had expanded well beyond its southeastern boundaries into California, Arizona, Nevada, Kansas, Texas, Illinois, and other major venues. The Daytona Speedway is only one of about a dozen speedways in the NASCAR series—not to mention the hundreds of small track races sanctioned by the venture.

Organized stock car racing began in 1949, with races run on dirt tracks and on the beach at Daytona. In 1949, NASCAR sanctioned 87 races. By 1968, it sanctioned over a thousand; and by 1972, 1,700 races at 97 tracks—with attendance estimated at over 8.5 million.

Those were huge numbers. So where were all the market-ers? (Here's where the NASCAR blindness theme comes in.) Advertisers must have perceived the primarily middle-class NASCAR audience as a bunch of back-country folks, who cer-tainly weren't "their people," not the kind of people their high-falutin clients should be investing their ad dollars in.

There is a market for every product, but who is to say that people outside that market might not be interested in what you're selling, as well? Could this be why general merchandise stores became popular, and stores like Target and Wal-Mart draw such large crowds?

I watched many a race from the press area with Steve Waid, one of the foremost NASCAR journalists. He has covered the sport for more than 35 years, and I was curious as to how he saw the situation. Here's what he told me:

They [advertisers] didn't know any better and were virtu-ally disinterested. Before its peak, NASCAR was simply a regional sport that didn't make the national radar very often. It didn't seem to have the audience the brands wanted. They seemed to think that most sponsors were automotive after-market products (which they were), and that other products weren't compatible with the fans. Fans, by the way, were considered little more than auto buffs and T-shirt wearers who drank beer. And [to advertisers] the audience was com-paratively small. No bang for the brand buck at all, or so they thought.

It's not that the brands so much missed the boat. They never thought the boat was there. The only argument against them is that they never sought to cultivate the market, rather than simply exploit it, and they never understood, or were told about, the fierce brand loyalty NASCAR fans have always had. That would come later.

When it comes to selling a product, the world is your oyster; just get it out there. Serve and support your customer. Gain loyalty by expanding your reach. Again, it all comes down to building that community.

In a recent blog post for *AdWeek*, Alan Wolk wrote about NASCAR blindness, adding this really solid statement:

> NASCAR blindness causes us to ascribe our tastes and preferences to the rest of America. So we're both shocked and dismissive when focus group participants in Des Moines don't know that Pinot Grigio is a type of wine—let alone a dry Italian white one. Or when they need to see the word "next" adjacent to the right-facing arrow on a Web page to figure out what it is they're actually supposed to do with said arrow. Here again, it doesn't make them stupid. It just makes them different. And if what we're creating is specifically aimed at them, it makes us stupid if we insist on talking to them in a language they can't relate to.

Respect your prospective buyer; you never know where they will come from or who they might know. Customer service is the most effective form of marketing.

When I was the brand-new kid in fashion advertising at the *Los Angeles Daily News*, Saks Fifth Avenue opened a new store. The store was in Woodland Hills, which at the time was a sleepy-bedroom, high-demographic community in the San Fernando Valley, very close to Chatsworth, a horse-owning community. The new general manager of the store assembled his floor staff for several conferences. One staff meeting consisted of a customer service speech. The GM told the employees not to judge the customer by what she is wearing or how she looks. A customer in cowboy boots and a plaid shirt is to be respected as much as the one who comes in wearing designer clothes. Either one may be able to afford anything she wants in the store.

People have to be reminded.

The lesson, of course, as in the NASCAR story, is that if you prejudge and fail to respect your prospective customer, you may lose many a sale. Likewise, if you prejudge your customers, your mode of customer service may not appeal to them or satisfy their needs. Look at your product, decide who would use it, *then* decide how you can best make your customers happy.

9

Platforms to Enhance the Experience

Although it's critically important, all this outreach to serve your customers takes precious time. Fortunately, the same technology that brought businesses online can also make your life easier. In this chapter I describe some popular tools and shortcuts that can make your interaction with your customers run a lot more smoothly than might seem possible initially.

All of the books I've written convey a recurring message for small business: Save time, save money. From the years I spent in my own business, I've discovered there are many tools available to help businesses *without* spending a fortune; and while inexpensive is good, free is even better.

Why not start small when you're beginning your efforts to institute your online outreach? Though jumping in with both feet using an expensive, enterprise-level program can seem appealing, you may find yourself caught in a learning curve that takes far more time to climb than you care to invest.

That said, the lure of the "30-day free trial" for a platform *is* tempting. And vendors know that once you've devoted hours to setting up an application—possibly incorrectly if you're doing it for the first time—you'll probably feel invested enough to carry on with their service. The most flexible platform vendors offer a free miniversion that you can try, or a basic setup online demo that can save you both time and energy.

The Internet is packed with numerous startup services boasting great new ideas and applications; they may come from tried-and-true net programmers or entrants to the arena. Since your time to play around with tools is limited, you need to be judicious with your choices. As you probably know from your own experience, just because people have great ideas doesn't mean that they always follow through. An online service that looks good today may not even be around tomorrow. So it's important that you first vet any service you plan to use. See if it has been in business for a while; Google its history; and ask for references if you plan on investing your time.

There are various categories you might want to investigate when planning your own online customer service outreach. Knowing where and how to do your research efficiently is more than half the battle.

Keeping Up with the Leaders

Reaching out to your customers shouldn't be a mystery. It's always sensible to keep up with big business transitions. For example, remember that Nordstrom—a company lauded for its exceptional customer service—is slipping out of the top 10 in this category? I'm not sure why this is occurring, but it serves as a reminder that customer perception of your service is based on what you are doing *today*. Resting on your laurels is never a good idea. The who, what, when, where, and why of your industry needs to be monitored—*especially* when it comes to customer service.

There are a couple of top places to check for the current leaders in customer service:

National Retail Federation (www.nrf.com). This venerable organization, founded in 1911, is the leading voice for all retail businesses (mentioned in Chapter 1 in regard to its annual Peter Glen Award). Members come from all retail formats including department, specialty, discount, catalog, Internet, and independent stores; chain restaurants; drug and grocery stores; as well as key trading partners of retail goods and services.

The NRF is a powerful organization that represents more than 1.6 million U.S. retail companies, more than 24 million employees, and 2009 sales of $4.1 trillion. In 1996, it formed a digital division solely for online retail, at www.shop.org. You can visit the NRF web sites regularly for news and information that will affect your business on a day-to-day basis.

For the past five years, the NRF's nonprofit foundation has presented the American Express-sponsored Customers' Choice Awards to honor retailers across all channels and formats that demonstrate superior customer service. The awards are based on a survey conducted by consumer marketing intelligence firm BIGresearch. The survey polls more than 8,000 consumers, to gauge consumer attitudes toward retailers' customer service and to provide a list of the top customer service retailers.

Consumers are asked the following open-ended question: "Thinking of all the different retail formats (store, catalog, Internet, or home shopping), which retailer delivers the best customer service?" The winners are announced each year at the National Retail Federation's annual conference.

Table 9.1 lists the top 10 retailers since the award's inception. Studying the rise and fall of the various brands portrays a very clear history of retailing in the past five years. You can see the movement to e-commerce, and how some major retailers have "lost their grip." Studying this comparison also allows you to see which companies are keeping up and improving. Finally, "shopping" the top 10 enables you to witness firsthand just what it is that makes them excel.

STELLAService (www.stellaservice.com). An up-and-coming site, this is the first and only company that covers the online customer service arena exclusively. STELLA Service, launched in March 2010, is already making a name in new media for its STELLA Ratings.

As cofounder and CEO Jordy Leiser explains, "STELLA Service was created to provide consumers with an unprecedented level of transparency around the customer service performance of online businesses." The organization guides consumers to e-commerce sites that maintain the highest-quality customer care. For each online business evaluated, STELLA conducts usability tests, orders (and returns) several products, and engages in over a dozen interactions with each company's customer service representatives, via phone, e-mail, and Live Chat.

STELLA evaluated the online customer service of the top 150 largest online retailers for 2010 (which can be found on its site), as measured by annual revenue. Based on these

Table 9.1 NRF/American Express Customers' Choice Survey: Top 10

	2009	2008	2007	2006	2005
1	L.L. Bean	L.L. Bean	L.L. Bean	Amazon.com	Nordstrom
2	Overstock.com	Overstock.com	Zappos.com	Nordstrom	Coldwater Creek
3	Zappos.com	Zappos.com	Amazon.com	L.L. Bean	Marshall Field's
4	Amazon.com	Amazon.com	Overstock.com	Overstock.com	Kohl's
5	QVC	Lands' End	Blair	Lane Bryant	Boscov's
6	Coldwater Creek	Newegg.com	Lands' End	Boscov's	REI
7	HSN	JC Penney	Coldwater Creek	Kohl's	JC Penney
8	Lands' End	QVC	Nordstrom	REI	Lane Bryant
9	JC Penney	Coldwater Creek	Lane Bryant	Lands' End	Best Buy
10 (tie)	Nordstrom	Nordstrom	Newegg.com	Macy's	Eddie Bauer
10 (tie)	Kohl's				

149

ratings, the top five companies for 2010 are Zappos.com, Diapers.com, Blue Nile, Staples, and L.L. Bean; Amazon .com, Crutchfield, Apple, Sears, and REI rounded out the top 10.

STELLA's methodology for ranking each business is to evaluate online tools, shipping and returns, and customer support. A perfect score is 100. Companies rated Elite (90–100) or Excellent (80–89) are awarded the STELLA Service Seal; the site also rates sites as Approved (70–79) or Not Recommended (below 70). Although STELLA's services are new, I'm sure it's worthwhile to follow its blog and rankings for the latest trends in online customer service.

Study the Demographics

In Chapter 8 on demographics, I highlighted the need to sort out the best ways to "speak" with the different generations that are using your products or services. Should your approach vary from social media site or e-commerce platform?

You need to get current information on users, to stay ahead of your competition. The great news is that you don't have to spend a fortune on high-end services, because the information is free. So how do you know which sites your customers are using most? Here's an option: Google partnered with DoubleClick to form Ad Planner. It's a site that helps you place your Web ads with laser accuracy so that they reach the appropriate audience for your advertising. Aside from planning ad budgets, it's a great way to find up-to-the-minute demographics on popular Web sites.

By simply signing in to Ad Planner you can access statistics on the number of unique visitors, page views, and other data for millions of Web sites from more than 40 countries. You can regularly check the site to get current monthly demographic information on gender, education, age, and household income on the sites you use for outreach or research. Find this very handy tool at www.google.com/adplanner.

Tools to Run Your Small Business Like a Big Brand

Anyone who is building a business should know about a company called 37signals, a developer of Web-based applications to help your business take control of the overwhelming issues you face on a daily basis.

At 37signals, the goal is to simplify useful software products. You don't have to download a thing; the company's applications are hosted on its systems on the Web (in the "cloud"), with no software for you to download to your system. By keeping the data on the Internet, anyone in your business can access your portal from any computer, anywhere. Best of all, the products available at 37signals.com start at $24 a month; and there are free starter versions for very small businesses.

Since the focus here is on customer service, I also have to recommend one of 37signal's apps, Highrise (highrisehq.com). It allows you to easily keep track of contacts—vendors, customers, and more. It's a robust communication tracking tool that boasts a variety of users, from one-person shops to enterprise-level businesses.

The longtime darling of customer relation management software is Web site Salesforce.com. It's a huge program with lots of options—in fact, this site is probably more than you need right now, but worth knowing about for the future. Salesforce .com recently launched a new version that operates in the cloud. Though it provides comprehensive service, you may be biting off more than you can chew, or can truthfully afford.

Highrise may be the preferable option here, as it's similar to Salesforce but much more compact, intuitive, and reviewed as easy to use. The least expensive version starts at $24 a month, but the free version (2 users, no files, 250 maximum contacts), is a great starter app. I established a free account for my business on Highrise and set it up in just a few minutes. All of my questions were answered right there on the setup page; there was no need to attend a webinar. It was perfect for someone like me (and so many others!) with no time to spare.

One of the things that especially impressed me about Highrise was the note that appeared on the screen: "You have selected the free plan. There is no time limit on the free plan—you can use it for free as long as you'd like. You can always upgrade to a paying plan later if you need file uploading, more cases, more contacts, etc." Nice.

According to the site, "Highrise is a great way for business to keep track of who talked to whom, what was said, and what needs to happen next." And it's true: It does *all* of that, incredibly well. You can take a look at Highrise in action in a minute-long video on the Web site at http://highrisehq.com/tour.

Customer Service Tools for Your Web Site

Consider the design of your own Web site: How accessible are you to your customers? Are you giving them access to any services, or are you merely asking for an order and nothing else? If all you do is put up merchandise for sale—or promote your items with search engine optimization and wait for the money to roll in—then you're not providing any sort of service to your customers. (And, no, accepting PayPal payments doesn't count.)

It is important to personalize your Web site with a personal message, Frequently Asked Questions (FAQs), contact information, and timely updates. Make sure that the information on your site is written in an accessible, conversational tone. Stay away from jargon and language that sounds good but doesn't actually say anything concrete. Since you've got a pretty good handle about what your customer is looking for, use direct terms that are in common use with your audience.

The purpose of the FAQs page is to answer your customer's questions about the process of dealing with your company. Make it real; show that your organization is composed of real people and that you have a clear and understandable message. Take a photo of yourself, your staff (even if it's your family), and put it on the page. People love to see who they are doing business with. One of the best examples on the Web can be found at www.thinkgeek.com/help (see Figure 9.1). ThinkGeek takes a whimsical view of the world, and it's reflected on its Help page and in its customer community outreach.

Oh, and about that picture? Don't make it one of those overly stylized, posed images of you and/or your staff clad in business suits—you know, the ones that look like they should be in a frame on a 1980s Chamber of Commerce wall. If you're a woman, don't get overly made up then have a photo taken at the local mall glamour studio. And if you're a small company, you can add a personal touch by *including* a picture of your pet as part of the staff. (Zappos does it.) People love pictures of dogs. I used to have a snap of my dog, Skip, in a shipping box, dubbed as Chief Shipping Inspector.

Show the pictures you plan to use to a friend and colleagues (or post them on your site and send me the link). If the photo doesn't elicit a smile from friends when they see it, it probably doesn't accurately portray you. Give it another shot, and remember, be you, and be real.

Most common customer (that's you!) queries

Order Status
Has my order shipped yet?
When will I receive my order?
What shipping address did I use?

International Orders
Shipping outside of the US?
Need info on duties and taxes?

Returns & Exchanges
Need to return an item?
Looking for our return policy?

Size Charts

My Account
How do I change my password or email?
How do I change subscription options?

Contact Us
1-888-GEEK STUFF (1-888-433-5788)
703-293-6299
Order via Phone: Every Day, 7am - 11pm EST
Customer Service: Mon - Fri, 9am - 7pm EST

☒ E-mail Customer Service for Help

Other helpful information

New Customers
New customers looking for general information should
start here.

Ordering
How to order, payment methods, address verification,
taxes and other order-related questions.

Product Information
If you have a question about our products, they may be
answered here!

Shipping
Looking for info on our shipping policies and methods?

Gift Options

Rewards Program (Geek Points)
Frequent shoppers can earn discounts and freebies by
joining our Geek Points program.

Newsletter & Catalog
We send out cool emails and catalogs. Get more
information and sign up here.

About Us
Learn about the monkeys, humans, and dogs behind
ThinkGeek!

Affiliate Program
Link to us and earn money using our affilate program.

Other FAQs

Figure 9.1 Timmy the monkey is a charming icon for a customer
service rep, don't you think?

Connecting, Contacting, and Feedback

On your information page, you should provide, at the very least,
contact information that will help the customer (and you) speed
up the conversation. Your Web hosting company may have a free
tool available on its site that you can use to set up your contact

and feedback form. If nothing is available, you can always check the Web.

I ran a Google search on "free html contact form" and found over a million links to free forms. If you're a bit squeamish about putting in HyperText Markup Language (HTML), ask a computer-savvy friend (or his or her kids) to do it. If your site is set up on WordPress, you'll find several widgets to easily set up a basic one.

I talked in Chapter 3 about the various Live Chat options for your site. Take a look at some of those options. Either of the leading providers, such as Skype or Google, will work. Both are free, and, they offer professional-looking, customizable buttons on their sites, as well as give you instructions on how to insert the supplied code onto your pages.

After signing up for a Skype account, simply choose to show your status on Skype (as to whether or not you're available), and the button will change from one option to another: Call me, Skype me, Online but not available, Offline, I'm not available, or I'm away (see Figure 9.2). Keep in mind that there's no reason to ever be "away." For a tiny fee, Skype will forward all queries to your landline or mobile. If you're really not available at the moment, then whoever is trying to reach you can also leave you a voicemail.

Google Voice is another professional call solution that I use every day. Voice differs from other similar applications because you receive a phone number. You can choose almost any area code or any city for the number that is assigned to you, and that

Figure 9.2 Skype offers many options for your Web site buttons. These are just a couple of them.

you will end up giving out by putting it on your business cards, e-mail signature, and so forth. The number can be configured to ring on any of your registered phone lines: mobile, office, store, or home. If you don't answer, your voicemail is stored in the cloud, where you can access it from any Web browser or phone. If you choose, Google Voice will transcribe your voice-mail and send you an e-mail message with the transcribed text. You can also receive a text message notifying you when a message is waiting for you.

For customer service purposes, Google Voice has Web site widgets that can forward calls to any of your numbers or directly to a prerecorded voicemail that you've prepared specifically for your customers. You can also have custom voicemail greetings for different incoming phone numbers, and use features like call merging and free domestic calls. The only charges involved for the service are for international calls.

Figure 9.3 Notice how you can set up the widget to ring any or all of your numbers when a call comes in.

If you want to return calls from your mobile or place calls displaying your Google Voice number in Caller ID, it's no problem. Although there are downloadable apps for the BlackBerry and Android, Google Voice has a Web-based version that accesses the service on an iPhone, Windows, Palm WebOS, or other device. To take advantage of the Web version, go to the mobile site at m.google.com/voice. If you don't have an unlimited text plan, you can use the mobile site to send Short Message Service (SMS) messages for free.

Google purchased a Skype lookalike Voice-over Internet Protocol (VoIP) service called Gizmo5, which is a provider of Internet-based calling software for mobile phones and computers. So if, for some reason, you want to use both combined, you will be able to do so in the very near future.

Phew! With all of that functionality there's pretty much *no* excuse left for failing to connect online to your customers and community.

Frequently Asked Questions and Support Community

When you shop or visit many of the major sites of any industry, you'll no doubt see a link to a community area. This can feature anything from a linked list of FAQs, with interactive answers, to a full-blown community of numerous links and active participation from site visitors.

Once again, how you design yours is a choice for you to make. You need to decide based on your time and money constraints; however, it's a real plus to have a community service area. You might just be able to handle Facebook, Twitter, and a blog to accomplish the same thing.

Some people link a ning.com platform for a business social network. The most basic version is very inexpensive and has been used successfully by lots of established Web sites. You can also build in your own community from GetSatisfaction.com, which can integrate into your own site. It's an easy-to-manage, lightweight option for building customer interaction. It's based on customer-to-customer support, which is often perceived as a more organic approach. It affords the benefit to publicly display issues you are currently addressing and those you've already solved.

GetSatisfaction.com was originally launched to solve a problem that the founders had with their original business, Valleyschwag. They knew the pain of delivering customer service via e-mail but, in contrast, had had amazing experiences answering questions in public and via their blog. The outcome was the platform they now offer—which is more results-oriented and social than the alternate ways of dealing with customer issues.

Get Satisfaction (getsatisfaction.com) offers a free small-business solution to help you get started on the site, an ideal way for you to enhance your customer service by allowing open comments and engaging your customers via simple FAQs. As you grow, the site offers many graduated steps, so you can upgrade to a more robust platform.

I originally learned about the site's unique features from Paul Hopkins, previously at easyJet.com (@easyJetCare on Twitter), an airline based in the United Kingdom that carries more passengers than any other British airline. The most significant fact about easyJet is that 98 percent of its bookings are placed online. The company uses a simple Get Satisfaction solution on its FAQ page, which displays a clickable listing of FAQs and a keyword search to the airline's online solution database.

Paul had a few good tips to share in terms of the benefits of using a simple version of FAQs on your site:

When writing FAQs, write the content, then halve it—then halve it again. It may seem rather direct, but [most] people don't have time to read lots of text. Since I have used this approach, self-serve rates and customer satisfaction related to the helpfulness of FAQs have gone up. Also, ensure that the customer service team—not the Web content team—manages the FAQs.

Use Web chat on FAQs; [since it's a place where] people would usually send an e-mail, this will reduce your volume of e-mails. It is also stops e-mail Ping-Pong, as the first e-mail is cheap and the second is expensive, [because] the agent has to read all previous content and then write the same answer in another way.

FAQs pages and customer-supported help can be cost-saving for your business as it grows. GetSatisfaction.com's full community-based platforms are being used by top companies like Twitter and Starbucks.

Handling the Support Issues

Once you're aware of your company's issues, having a platform to handle queries from a browser, which becomes your own service desk, is a great idea. For Web businesses that have to handle many online requests, help desk software can be the answer. This way, you can respond promptly to customer inquiries, complaints, and service queries.

There are quite a few help desk options, among them Zendesk, which is widely used and has become a popular platform. It provides an integrated help desk and customer support portal. Quite a few people integrate the Zendesk support with either the Salesforce or Get Satisfaction community solution.

This help desk software is Web based and covers customer support, trouble tickets, and a knowledge base. It's not free, but the powerful Zendesk has a starter package for $9 a month, with a 30-day free trial. It gets more expensive when you add more operators, but to start this could be a solid platform. Learn more at www.zendesk.com.

I've also been beta-testing Hy.ly, a new Twitter monitoring service specifically designed for customer care, which should be out of beta very soon. With Hy.ly not only can you monitor mentions, but also manage, respond, and organize your Twitter stream on one easy online interface. Different from Zendesk, Hy.ly's single system gives you one screen for all your work. It has an integrated data view where you can monitor, collaborate, and produce action tickets in a single workflow. Learn more about the service at www.hy.ly.

Blogging for Your Business

Speaking of community, even if your Web site is designed for e-commerce, building a community will give users something to read and peruse, other than the items you offer for sale. This leads to the idea of a blog—or at the very least, some regularly updated educational pages on your product or industry—fun facts and interesting info that you and the community will enjoy. *This* is the kind of material that keeps people coming back.

Remember, you're not the only one on the Web selling your product—not by a long shot. Buyers are attracted not only by price; they care about your service, their relationship to your company, and the content you present.

A recent study from Internet marketing company HubSpot revealed data from more than 1,500 businesses that indicated your Web site will be indexed by search engines far more frequently if you do some sort of blogging than if you don't (see Figure 9.4).

Why is this important? When you signal authority to search engines, it increases your chances of being found by prospective customers in those very search engines. These are people who are interested in your product and message.

You can either set up these pages as part of your Web site or present them as a standalone blog. Whichever you choose, your blog should be part of your site's top level navigation links—and your customer should *know* that you have a blog.

So how do you start? Again, your Web-hosting company probably has a template enabling you to add a blog to your site. If it doesn't, start one from a free platform. Take a look at sites

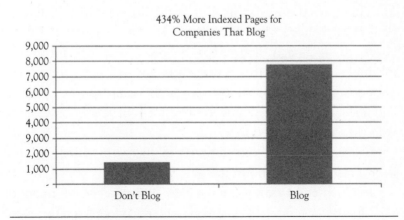

Figure 9.4 HubSpot's data makes it crystal clear as to why you should blog, in one form or another.

like WordPress (wordpress.org) and Blogger (blogger.com) to get started. But keep in mind that "free" doesn't always mean totally without cost. For example, a Google search on the term "free blog" will produce many possible options. A lot of respected platforms are free and give beginners a good deal of help, and some of these really stand out from the rest. You'll learn a lot.

Now, for the nonfree part: Blogger (which is run by Google) offers a custom top level where you can blog for a mere $10 a year. Though it's not free, it's not a bad deal, considering it offers quite a bit of storage. You can begin to blog with the free version and upgrade to a custom URL later—a transition that Blogger makes fairly easy. Switching your blog to a custom domain through Google maintains both your page rank and search engine status. However, be aware that search engines have a duplicate content penalty that can affect your ranking if you try to redirect a Blogger blog merely by using a *meta redirect*. A meta redirect is accomplished when your customer types in one site's URL and gets redirected to another through meta tags in the site's HTML.

There are those who support both Blogger and WordPress, and most believe that WordPress is the more professional alternative—though Blogger has its fans, too. It is better to not ask for advice about this, since everyone will have their own opinions. Better to do your own research, compare your options, and make the decision that works best for you, your business, and your time constraints.

Currently, the basic differences between Blogger and WordPress are those shown in Table 9.2.

In Chapter 4 I gave you some ideas of the sort of information you can include on your blog, so along with the information here, you really have no reason not to begin blogging. And, of course, don't forget to link your blog posts on your Twitter stream.

Table 9.2 Blogger versus WordPress Features

Options	Blogger	WordPress
Themes	Free; editable, or ability to install a third-party theme	No customization on the free platform
Static pages	Up to 10 additional static pages	Static pages are listed in separate menus
Domain name	Free domain mapping	None on free platform
Image storage	1GB; more if you sign up for Picasa	3GB
Ease of use	Beginner	Medium/advanced

Monitoring Your Web Mentions

I know this might seem like even more work, but if you have any sort of online presence, then online is the first place you'll hear of your successes and your failures. You've got to keep your ears open to what people are saying about you on the Web, because today's social media platforms and users can spread information on you or your business within seconds. So when it comes to keeping tabs on the online mentions about your business, you'll need to monitor the Web, then address complaints or negative reviews as quickly as possible.

I've tested a wide variety of monitoring products and offer my recommendation for small business in the next section. Note that I only advocate sites that I really like personally, and that have performed well for me and my business. When it comes to Web notifications, I want a comprehensive view of exactly what is going on. It is best to find a program that does not require your customers to sign up before they can leave feedback or a review. If I visit a site with the intent to review, and discover that it requires me to sign up before I get to see the company's prices, I will leave the site without posting my review. That sort of marketing is very old school, and there are plenty of superior options available nowadays.

The one thing you must do immediately is set up a Google Alerts. Google Alerts monitors content on the Web based on a set of keywords you select. You can set up alerts about your products, your industry, or your city; but most importantly, you'll want set up alerts on your public name, your business, and your competition. To set up Google Alerts, go to www.google .com/alerts.

Table 9.3 Basic Shortcuts for More Accurate Searches

Command	Effect on Search	Example
No symbol, multiple words; e.g., *Mount Olympus*	Posts that include the words anywhere	*mount olympus* might return an Olympus camera or a mountain in Greece
Terms in quotes; e.g., *"mount olympus"*	Posts that have the exact phrase within the quotes	*"mount olympus"* will return references to a mountain in Greece
OR; e.g., *mount* OR *olympus*	Posts with either of the words appears	Returns posts with any mentions of *mount* or *olympus*
Minus sign; e.g, mount–olympus	Posts that have one word but not the other	Posts including *mount*, but not *olympus*
near within*; e.g, *near* athens *within:* 15mi	Tweets from a specific location	Tweets sent within 15 miles of athens (GA, or Greece)
since*; e.g.,: ouzo *since* 2010–05–15	Tweets on keyword sent after a certain date	Tweets about an ouzo party sent after 2010–05–15

*Twitter-specific search operands

Google Alerts is a basic tool: It only "scrubs" the Google search. The comprehensive alert will let you know if your keywords appear in the top 10 results in news and blogs, and the top 20 results for a Google Web search. Your results can get to you through an RSS feed or via e-mail. You also can set the option as to how many e-mails you receive from Google daily; and when it comes to your name and your business, I recommend you set the frequency to "as it happens."

Table 9.3 gives you a few tricks for using search engines when you are looking for how your business is represented online. There are commands that are used to combine keywords to broaden or narrow a search, and using these in your searches will make them faster and more accurate.

One of the most important commands to remember in Table 9.3 is the use of quotation marks. This is vital when it comes to finding names of people or businesses. Also keep in mind that searches on any platform are not case-sensitive.

Social Media Searches

Setting up Google Alerts is great for beginners, but in order to really get a complete picture of what your customers are saying online, you'll have to go to a site or use a tool that aggregates searches from all over the Web. (Remember, currently, Google Alerts mostly finds things in the top 10.)

I have found the following sites to be very useful:

SocialMention.com. Searches various sites and presents graphics for each search to indicate sentiment, strength, passion, and reach. Though the site has lots of nice features, unfortunately you cannot combine multiple searches in one pass. If you have one or two searches, you might be better off signing up for an ongoing RSS feed from the site.

Socialsearch.com. This social search includes Yelp. It might be a good site for restaurants and other brick-and-mortar businesses to check out.

Spindex: At the time of this writing, Spindex was still in beta. From Microsoft Fuse Labs, it allows you to access and interact with your social networks, view trends from your friends, and see related info from Bing—literally, *everywhere* you click. Spindex proactively finds useful articles and information based on your interest in your friends' messages and comments. Time will tell whether this will be a new killer app.

Twiogle.com: As the name might suggest, this is a combination of Twitter and Google. Clickable tabs allow specific searches.

Twitter: If you just want to find your company or personal name in Twitter, you can use Twitter Search to search from your home page—or just go to search.twitter.com.

Whostalkin.com: This is a pretty slick interface; however, searches done on different platforms need to be conducted individually, so it can take a lot of time. Still, it's pretty thorough and worth checking out.

Finding People to Follow on Twitter

It can be tough staring at that blank page once you've set up your Twitter account. To help you get past that point, you need to visit one or both of these sites: Twellow (twellow.com) and WeFollow (wefollow.com). These are Twitter directories that categorize members by keywords. Mr. Tweet (mrtweet.com) is another helpful site, with a "who should I follow" link. Once you've found a good group of people to follow, the site suggests others that relate to them. It's a little complex, but very thorough. Simply visit these sites and input keywords that describe your business, industry, city, or products/services. You'll receive suggestions of who to follow, so you can start to build a fun group.

Remember: Don't go crazy! Keep in mind that Twitter has rules, and sets "follow limits" on accounts. Once you follow people, Twitter expects that certain numbers are going to follow you back. Once you hit 2,000 followers (the number may be different for your account), Twitter measures your percentage of follow-backs. You don't want to be labeled as a spammer, so understand that building a Twitter community is not going to happen overnight. Besides, who *really* needs to follow 2,000 people at a time?

Twitter also monitors all accounts for "aggressive following and follow churn"—in other words, repeatedly following and unfollowing large numbers of other users. The point is, you've got to give this tool time, and allow people to discover you. Remember that Twitter is a mutual conversation between people; it's not a broadcasting platform.

When people follow you, if at all possible before following back, click to their Twitter pages, read their bios, and look at their tweets. Following a spammer or someone who is not interested in conversing is a waste of your time and bandwidth, and could damage your good name.

Managing Your Twitter Stream

Once you are following and being followed by a few hundred people, you're going to wonder why you ever followed back so many people. An important element of social media engagement is inclusion and making people feel part of a collaborative community.

You've got to use a tool that can help you isolate your closest friends, family, and Twitter friends so that you don't miss any of their comments. You can't converse if you don't know what they are talking about!

When you look at a Twitter stream in your browser, you'll be able to see which software your friends are using to manage their tweets—it's in the pale, gray type below the tweet. Check out what other people like yourself are using; that may give you an idea of what's best to use. Also, bear in mind that the way you work may not equate to your friends' style of working, so be sure to try out the different platforms before deciding on one.

There are several very simple applications available for managing your Twitter tweets and friends. For a single computer, check out TweetDeck or Seesmic, both widely used and well respected. You can follow on your monitor lists, keyword searches, your mentions, direct messages, and your full home stream all at once.

Larger platforms that also work well when you have several people tweeting from the same account are HootSuite, Hy.ly, and CoTweet. These applications are very robust and are full of automation.

When it comes to serving your customer online, putting systems in place early on will make your transition far easier. That's why many of these sites offer starter packages. The bigger your business gets, the more you'll need to use these online platforms to organize your outreach.

10

Engaging Your Employees as Brand Ambassadors

As far as customers are concerned, the most important aspect of any company is the experience they have, *not* the tangible attributes of a company's product or service. Your employees are your first-level, frontline customer service representatives, online or in person. When they discuss your business with a friend, post to their blog, or tweet on Twitter, they can—in mere seconds—make your company shine, or seriously damage your business's reputation.

Every single staff member who makes your business run on a daily basis has a hand in your customer service approach. How your employees feel about you, as their leader, and the culture in which they work, will have a lot to do with whether or not they take pride in their work. If they have a positive attitude when speaking to or connecting online with customers, they will put their best foot forward. They will want to be sure customers are happy with their contact. Customer loyalty will be uppermost in their minds. So hiring employees who care—who are as emotionally invested in your dream as you are—can make all the difference in your success or failure.

As a small businessperson, you are your own human resources department. You have to hire and fire based on your instincts as to how well a given job is being done; and it's never easy. The people I worked with in my own company over the years understood customer service. There was nothing we wouldn't do to keep our clients happy. There was never a client request that was too impossible or too outrageous.

No client was too small. If they paid the fees, we were at their disposal. Collier Company, Inc. was nothing without our clients, and because of this we never lost a single one due to bad service. I was the employee for my clients, and my employees were there to help me make the magic happen. Customer magic goes on 24/7; a "wow" only lasts a moment or two.

That's what it's all about: In order for you to make the magic happen for *your* customers, you need loyal employees who support you. And while finding employees who think like you do and have the same level of commitment to customer service is tough, keeping them happy is even tougher.

This is, however, another circumstance where small businesses have an advantage over larger companies. Bigger corporations have lots of layers in the ranks, which has a tendency to cause some detachment between top level and worker bees. During the years I worked for a corporation, there was often an apparent "us versus them" mentality.

In a recent episode of the CBS television show *Undercover Boss*, CEOs from several well-known major American corporations went "undercover" to perform low-level jobs at their own organizations. The CEOs who connected best with their employees while undercover were the ones who had worked their way up to the corporate level. They exhibited how important it was to be humble—that there's a benefit in knowing how a business works from the bottom up.

This is truly the best way to learn. As a small-business owner there is a benefit to being familiar with every aspect of your business. Don't just delegate to and rely on others to complete certain tasks; do them yourself. Humility in all aspects of business gives one the best perspective, and the opportunity to "feel the pain" of others.

Like customer loyalty, gaining employee loyalty is another art form. Develop a culture where your employees feel that they are part of something bigger, and not merely another cog in the wheel. This means you need to check your ego at the door and lead by example.

I worked for several different companies during college and in my early professional years. One position was with a small company (about 200 employees) that was run by a hands-on president who worked in the trenches right alongside us; we saw him every day. Thus, we regarded him as more than just a figurehead. This was a company where the employees inspired management; with all of us working toward a common goal, we developed a sense of camaraderie. As low-level a job as mine was, my coworkers' morale made it a genuinely positive experience for me.

At the other end of the spectrum was a contract job I had at a family-run business that—after clear success in its field—hired a small group of MBAs to take over and bring it to the next stage. While the firm *did* end up making more money, relationships with both customers and staff suffered. Why? Because management was making decisions based on the bottom line rather than on people.

What do these two opposite examples show?

The trend is fairly obvious: It seems that humanity tends to drift once a company becomes multilayered.

At both of those companies, employees received bonuses, so money wasn't the issue. The personal investment will permeate a workplace when management is an active part of the team. When victories at all levels are lauded by all, employees will care about the success of both the business and their colleagues. Employees who take their work personally are those who—online or offline—will have your company's best interests at heart.

I asked Amanda Hite (@sexythinker on Twitter), CEO and founder of Talent Revolution, Inc., if she, as a business owner, had any tips for teaching good customer service. Here's what she had to say:

> First, I have to teach them to think differently about "who" our customer is. Our customer is our community, which stretches far beyond the current clients who have retained our services. They are all of the people that exist within the reach of the community we've built, and reach on- and offline. Part of that community is made up of our existing clients, but many of them are potential or future clients and/or people who influence what is being said to others about our brand. Serving the people who impact "word of mouth" and our future is equally as important as serving the people who are working with us in the moment.
>
> Second, and most importantly, I have to model the behavior. I have to demonstrate through my actions that I maniacally listen and *care* about our community on- and offline.
>
> The last thing is I have to teach is that "everything communicates," and set the standard that everything we do must communicate who we are and that we *care*. Be crystal clear about that outcome, but let each player on the team get there (and deliver that service) in [his or her] own unique way. That's what makes it authentic. And that authenticity

is what differentiates us and makes it matter to the customer. Ultimately, it's what lets them know we *care*.

Businesspeople are always shocked when faced with the statistics that have come to be common knowledge in so many of their industries. For example, as a small-business owner, how well do you know your bank? A J.D. Power and Associates study of 6,397 small businesses revealed that nearly 60 percent were never contacted by their financial institutions. And the only contact that about one-third had is with a bank teller. Would you believe that "small businesses" included those with $5 to $10 million in sales? That means that those lower-level bank employees are the *only* customer service connection to what are potentially *billions* of dollars. The attitude reflected by the tellers then becomes the bank's only visible customer service to many of its customers. That's a lot of weight to put on someone, so one would hope that the tellers love their jobs.

A friend of mine, a budding MBA at a top-level business school, completed an employee satisfaction analysis of a well-known corporation where he was once employed. Leaving out the external issues (e.g., declining economy, rising cost of living, and so on), the researchers focused on and uncovered many internal threats to employee morale, among them:

- Lack of communication between upper management and company employees is increasingly causing a divide, which is slowly eroding the company from the inside out.
- Lack of performance incentives is leading to overall employee dissatisfaction, complacency, and lack of innovation—which further deteriorates the company.
- Significant friction between upper management and company employees is becoming more commonplace. By focusing almost entirely on increasing profits and creating new avenues of

revenue for the future, executives have left the well-being of employees out of the picture.

- There is a dearth of incentives to push the company's employees forward in hard economic times. There was a general consensus among lower-level employees that the most talented workers do not feel that they're adequately rewarded or compensated for their hard work and efforts.

The research team that interviewed the top-level executives at the corporation was taken aback when talking to one senior director in particular. He discussed many of the opportunities and challenges that the company faces in the external environment, and talked about the image of the brand, revenue generation, changes in research methodologies, and the impact of social media. However, this senior director made no mention of the concerns pertaining to employee morale.

Bottom line? If employees who are interviewed cite declining job satisfaction as their primary concern, this points to the *true* threat facing the company.

The disconnects my friend found in the study hopefully are not occurring at your company. To prevent this from happening, on a regular basis, take time to reflect on the best practices you've established for running your business. Put yourself in the place of various employees, and try to understand their experience in your organization. Better yet? Talk to them.

A vital function of your job as company leader is to help employees understand that they are also your *brand ambassadors*. Your ability to keep your customers coming back is dependent on the sum of all of their positive interactions with your company. One small slip of the tongue, one unintended offense, or one sign of disrespect from one of your employees could send your customers running to your competitors.

The Forrester 2007 Customer Experience Index found that "customers want their interactions with companies to be useful, easy, and enjoyable." This translates to the need for all employees to ensure that in every decision they make, the customers' needs come first.

From "Absolutely, Positively Overnight" to "We Live to Deliver"

Those are Federal Express campaign taglines from 1978 to the present. Not only does the company at large mean them, but each and every employee believes in and lives them. There are only a select few companies that can say their corporate culture is one that fosters loyalty and that special kind of commitment. Federal Express stands out in this respect—and so is a lauded example of outstanding customer service.

In the dark days before documents flew through wireless connections, Federal Express provided a vital service for every business. My own company used local messenger services and—despite our comparably small size—sent and received packages through Federal Express several times a week.

Since the 1980s, only three different Federal Express couriers have picked up from and delivered to my business. After a few years, the first courier was promoted to a position in the FedEx hub in Memphis; and I had to bid farewell to the second, Mark, because my company moved. But to this day, he is still delivering to customers along the same route.

Mark was the courier who picked up my deliveries the day I FedEx-ed my first book contract back to the publisher. He sprinkled imaginary good-luck fairy dust on the envelope for me—and it worked! He's still driving his truck because he loves it—and his customers love him. He goes out of his way to serve them.

FedEx employees deliver great customer service both in their face-to-face interactions with their customers as well as with those online. Taking a look at the Federal Express example should cause us all to pause to think about how we can apply the same quality practices to our own businesses.

If, for example, you reach out to FedEx on Twitter about an issue with your delivery, you will no doubt quickly get a response from @FedExRobin, a wonderful, loyal employee whose job it is to reach out to customers on the Web. Robin fully embraces the Federal Express Employee Purple Promise: "I will make every FedEx experience outstanding." Every employee takes this oath to heart—throughout this very large company.

Robin was recently featured in an in-house employee poster series, which was proudly sent to me by another FedEx employee, along with the following message: "I wanted you to see how much the company celebrates its people. It's an aspirational culture, with examples of great service. So, hopefully, everyone can aspire to be like Robin."

An aspirational culture. Not only does this organization take the time and effort to praise its employees, it also presents three highly visible customer service employee awards, which have become legendary for their effectiveness:

- *The Five Star.* This award recognizes team members who have enhanced service and profitability and exemplified the spirit of teamwork. Managers nominate their team members for this annual award, the highest at FedEx.
- *Bravo Zulu.* The Bravo Zulu award, derived from the U.S. Navy signal meaning "well done," is distributed to individuals within FedEx for outstanding performance beyond normal job expectations. Managers reward employees for outstanding efforts and achievement on the spot. Rewards may include

"quick cash" bonuses, theater tickets, dinner gift certificates, and other gifts of similar value.

- *Purple Promise.* According to FedEx, "Couriers, pilots, meteorologists, customer service agents and package handlers are just a few of the team members who must execute flawlessly to deliver the award-winning service our customers expect. Team members who consistently deliver superior customer service and make each and every FedEx experience outstanding are eligible for the annual Purple Promise awards."

These awards are not merely pieces of paper, not to the company or its employees. They are esteemed honors, and are backed with tangible cash or rewards to make each one that much more special. Can you put together an awards program at your business? Based on your goals, why not develop a plan, right now, for rewarding employees who make a difference to the everyday operation of your business.

I spoke with FedEx's Sheila T. Harrell, vice president of Customer Service Operations about the Purple Promise. She said it was "a concept that we all live by each and every day." She, as does every FedEx employee I spoke to, maintains the promise as part of their day-to-day culture.

Sheila was awarded the Customer Service Institute of America's 2008 Customer Service Executive of the Year award, and I have never spoken to anyone more passionate about customer service. I mentioned to her that I appreciated (in a customer service incident) the level of detail the company goes through to make things right. She told me that detail and preparedness for the unexpected are important. Also, that "every call/chat/tweet/interaction is an opportunity to make a difference."

To get some real-world comments on what it's like to work at FedEx, I crowd-sourced my followers on Twitter to find current or past FedEx employees. I asked them to tell me about their time at FedEx. Here is a sampling of their remarks:

> I made some great "friends" from some of the customers. Was always happy to hear their voices on the phone!
>
> I'm a former FedEx Customer Service Agent . . . I actually miss that job!
>
> The things I learned while working @Fedex are things I've carried with me forever.
>
> I got a lot of Bravo Zulus while I was there. My dad was an Ops Mgr at a station too.

Getting Your Employees Invested

If you want your employees to be as invested as you'd like them to be in your company (without granting points or giving them actual ownership), keep these basics in mind:

1. *Spend time with your employees during work hours.* If you watch your staff performing daily tasks, you can be proactive about what needs changing—quickly. If, instead, you wait until problems occur, the issues may have metastasized throughout your office, store, or restaurant. Be sure to block out specific times to do this in your workday, and make sure it's different each time, so that you can observe the ongoing relationships during various flows throughout the day.

   - Encourage your employees to explore and engage in online social media communities. Remember, they are also the face of your company to all their friends and associates, as well as the customers they know. Provide guidelines, in the form of a Social Media Policy, so they will know any limits as to what they can, and cannot, make public. See the sidebar for an example.

Sample Social Media Policy

Here's how one of our nation's biggest companies handled its Social Media Policy.

Before taking on his responsibilities at Dell as director of Interactive Marketing Communications, my friend Adam Brown developed a three-page document outlining "Online Social Media Principles" for the Coca-Cola Company. Aside from designating a code for its online spokespeople, Coca-Cola also laid out specific principles for its associates. By taking a look at what Coca-Cola has deemed appropriate perhaps it will help you forge a similar code for your employees.

These principles are guidelines for online activities where employees may mention the company:

a. *"Adhere to the Code of Business Conduct and other applicable policies."* Coca-Cola established several policies regarding a company code of business conduct, information protection, and insider trading. All employees (from the CEO to interns) are to keep these in mind when publically mentioning they are employees of Coca-Cola.

b. *"You are responsible for your actions."* This reminds associates that they must exercise sound judgment and common sense in what they say online. They are the keepers of the company image.

c. *"Be a 'scout' for compliments and criticism."* The company realizes that the people in its employ are its "most vital assets for monitoring the social media landscape." Coca-Cola provides an in-house e-mail address that goes to in-house spokespersons, to forward any comments or concerns they observe online.

(continued)

(continued)

d. *"Let the subject matter experts respond to negative posts."* This stresses that should there be a possibly damaging post online, the post should be referred to those trained as online spokespeople.

e. *"Be conscious when mixing your business and personal lives."* The company recognizes that personal and business personas may intersect online. This is a reminder that everything that is posted online can be seen by anyone, at any time.

- Be confident that you've hired the right people, then allow them to be the face of your business online. Employees who are proud of where they work will want the world to love their company as much as they do.
- Listen to how your employees interact with each other and with your customers. Is there a clear leader? Do employees turn to one specific person for help; and if so, are they consulting with the right person? Often, a long-time employee with a lot of experience can become the sounding board for newer hires. If that's the case, be sure that person is in a supervisory position with the proper status (and pay). Otherwise, the voluntary management of the department may be interfering with the work he or she *should* be doing. People may be able to multitask, but as they say, "Jack of all trades, master of none." There will be something in the individual's workload that is suffering.
- Be on the lookout for an individual left out during the daily work or social interactions. Perhaps there is a personal or even social problem that may need to be addressed.

Carefully observe whether the person's solitude is self-imposed or if that individual is overwhelmed with his or her work and needs help.

- Listen to the tone that your employees use to communicate with one another. Is someone speaking down to others on his or her team? This is not just a human resources issue; this is something you should do because you care about your employees. Even a great employee may also be a company bully, and it's your job to see that everyone is treated with respect.

2. *Don't just listen, interact.* Sometimes you may think that you're interacting just by "being there," but you're not. Interaction requires mutual communication and reciprocal contact. Establishing a personal connection helps your employees feel that you are on their team, that you're not above or below anything they do, and that their words all have equal import to *you.*

   This sort of discourse allows you to discover what's important to your staff members, where their unique talents lie, and what their perspectives are. By discussing these matters, your employees become real people to you, and your interest in them shows that you care about them. This will encourage them to feel invested in you and your business. Your dialogue also will go a long way toward energizing your workplace and making it a happier place to be for all. Need some suggestions on exactly how to do this?

   - When socializing with employees, be sure to be complimentary when speaking to one employee about another. This positive attitude will be infectious.
   - Be sure that each and every employee receives praise at one time or another. If someone doesn't deserve an '"atta boy/girl" at some point, then he or she shouldn't be in your

employ. Heartfelt compliments give all human beings pride in their work. Dignity goes a long way.

- Rather than making comments, ask questions. This opens up the kind of conversations that you and your staff members need to have.
- If you see a new picture on someone's desk, or notice something different about the person, be sure to acknowledge it and encourage him or her to tell you a story.
- When you see someone struggling with a task, or appearing at all overwhelmed, ask if he or she could use some help. If you, yourself, can't help out at the moment, find someone who can.
- If appropriate for your business, set up a special e-mail address where just employees can contact *you*. Should an employee come up with a brilliant idea on his or her own time, that person can ping you with the thought and elaborate. Employees may feel more comfortable expressing their ideas via a written document, rather than discussing it in front of others.

3. *Hold regular, scheduled meetings.* Most of us aren't huge fans of meetings—especially those where nothing is accomplished—but establishing a structured time and place for such gatherings shows that you care enough to take out time from your day to be there for your team. The point of these meetings (aside from communicating procedural changes and instructions) is to elicit feedback from your staff. Never forget, they are in the trenches every day and may just have an insight or two that hasn't occurred to you. They may have observed something that just doesn't work quite right—something *you* believed was running like a Swiss clock. Likewise, because your staff is in direct communication with your customers, they can get lots of information from them about things that might not come your way.

An additional benefit of meeting with your employees regularly, aside from getting information, is that doing so allows them to become more comfortable talking to you. Permitting free-form discussion, and providing an open and transparent atmosphere, has many benefits.

What kind of discussions should you have at meetings?

- Ask for feedback on current policies and procedure. But don't allow this to become a time-wasting complaint session. Take notes and, most importantly, *listen*. Remember to follow up after you've had time to investigate any issues raised.

- Ask whether your staff has any insights on your competition. Their eyes and ears are out there, and they may be privy to some valuable information that might not readily come your way.

- Ask open-ended questions. Never ask anything that can be answered with a simple yes or no. Knowing that something is wrong is useless unless you know exactly what, why, and how you can possibly fix it.

- Answer a question with a question. Sometimes this is the best way to get to the heart of any matter. By doing so you can elicit more than just the question; you might also get an in-depth answer that provides a solution—and you come across as someone who actually cares and listens.

Although meetings are great for dealing with everyday Sturm und Drang, an annual outing can also go a long way toward building company morale, camaraderie, and loyalty. Why not sponsor a picnic at a local park, with games, and encourage your staff to bring their families?

4. *Give your employees the autonomy to act on their own.* Let them make their own decisions in times of customer service crises (within outlined parameters, of course). By doing so, you allow your employees to invest in their desire to see that

everything comes out okay. It also encourages group thinking that's focused on bettering the team.

You want your employees to realize they are responsible for their own successes and failures. Although they probably learn more when something doesn't go as planned, the lesson learned is for the greater good; especially if it comes as an endnote to a well-intentioned action. After all, experience is the best teacher.

To get the best from your employees, why not:

- Teach your crew some tricks of the trade. These may be the kind of things that they didn't learn in school or in their daily work. Give them the sort of pointers that can only be learned from many years of experience in your industry.

- Always share the spotlight with your employees and/or managers. If someone has a good amount of experience and some advice that he or she would like to share with the group, encourage that person to do so. Not only are you educating your employees, but you just might learn something new yourself. Also, if you receive a compliment from a customer, always be sure to credit the team for their effort.

- Let your employees know that you have faith in them and that it's okay to make a decision or take some risks on the fly. If they hear this from you, they'll know that you trust them.

5. *Keep your workplace as up to date as possible.* Investing in new equipment, maintenance, and training in fresh techniques or ideas shows your employees that you take pride in the company and them. Have you ever worked somewhere where the boss just let things fall apart? Many managers do. Some may feel that it's "not their job" to provide an enlightening, interesting place to work. (I know that's not you, of course; after all, you *are* reading this book.)

One final point here: Keep the basics in mind. Don't think of this effort as building "corporate culture" (although that seems to be the buzzword these days); think of it as you and your staff working toward a common goal—and making a team effort to reach it.

Adding a personal touch to your interactions with both your customers and employees will lead to greater success and happier lives for everyone. Pride in your business is a positive motivator.

11

Pioneers of Online Community

How They Did It

There are a very small number of big public companies that have made history on the Internet. That's because many of these big companies originated as someone's passion, or from a plan drawn on a kitchen table, or a concept launched out of a garage. With that kind of passion, you really need to care about your customer.

The Internet started with people, scientists, engineers, and educators, all looking for a way to collaborate without the clumsiness of telephones and snail-mail. Besides, as they figured out, several people joining in a conversation can make progress a lot faster than talking one-on-one. One of my favorite quotes on the topic is from Tim Berners-Lee, the computer scientist who invented the World Wide Web, in March 1989 (sorry, Al Gore). Berners-Lee wrote in his 2004 essay, "Weaving the Web" that:

> The Web is more a social creation than a technical one. I designed it for a social effect—to help people work together—and not as a technical toy. The ultimate goal of the Web is to support and improve our weblike existence in the world. We clump into families, associations, and companies. We develop trust across the miles and distrust around the corner.

Real people start small businesses in their homes, garages, or even in small rented offices. These small businesses can become whopping big businesses or stay pleasant, family-run enterprises for years. The transition is a major one, and doesn't suit everyone. The most successful people who make the transition don't lose their core values of customer and community.

The examples of the businesses in this chapter show you how you can take your idea farther than you ever dreamed. They describe people, just like you and me, who built something wildly successful out of a desire to "make a killing," yet kept respect for their customers a priority.

Internet social interaction started with Usenet, as early as 1980. Usenet was essentially a long list of classified interest newsgroups where people could join lively conversations and share facts and interests. (There are still plenty of stalwarts on this old system. If you want to check them out, go to www.octanews.com, www.altopia.com, or find them in Google Groups.)

Back then, when you bought a computer you were given a CD and pushed to join CompuServe or AOL as your first online venture. In those days, these services hosted lively chat rooms and interest groups, and if you were into computers, you were there.

At that time, I was a single mom running a fairly successful retail shopping center marketing business. When my daughter was asleep, I met and chatted with my online friends (very much like today, on Twitter). These were people from all over the country. There were many chat rooms and lots of interesting topics. Most of all, we met just to talk.

I had interested my daughter in the TV series *Star Trek*, and it had become something of a hobby for both of us, so I also checked out the *Star Trek* chat rooms. At the time I thought I might be able to monetize our hobby. In fact, I did, and built it into quite a business.

The *Star Trek* user groups were very lively in those days, featuring lots of chatter about TV shows, toys, and the unavailability of short-stocked action figures. My daughter enjoyed collecting these figures, and I had begun to purchase them from other members in the group, to fill her collection.

My daughter and I would spend Saturday mornings scouring the stores for the newest action figures. Eventually, I asked the members of the action figure community whether they would be interested in an e-mail auction that would end in a live auction in the chat room at the end of a week. They thought it was a great idea.

To begin, I sent out an e-mail with a list of items we had purchased at retail and put them up for my e-mail auction, with the starting bids at approximately what we'd paid. Each night I'd collect the responses and update the next-day's e-mail to go out with the new high bids. This went on for the full week. And then? The final live auction.

We all would meet in a chat room, our little community, and I'd type in each item with the current highest bid. People would raise the price until . . . going, going, gone. My daughter, sitting next to me, kept track of the bidders and the bidding on a notepad.

That might have been the beginning of a profitable new business, but AOL heard of my online venture and I received an e-mail letting me know that this sort of entrepreneurship was no longer allowed on AOL, and that if I continued, I would be banished from the service.

I sent an e-mail out to my online friends letting them know of the situation. It was pretty crushing. Even my tween daughter was disappointed that we were losing our business. So I searched the Web for another place to continue our little family-side enterprise.

Someone smarter than I, part of the online community, directed me to a relatively new site, AuctionWeb.com.

eBay—Née AuctionWeb

AuctionWeb was created by a brilliant young programmer, Pierre Omidyar, on Labor Day 1995, partly as a hobby and partly to practice programming for the Web. Initially, this tiny e-commerce site was run from a server in Omidyar's spare bedroom in his townhouse.

Back then, when only well-connected insiders made profits on the Internet, Omidyar had different ideas. Like many young guns of the day, he felt that financial and commerce markets should be free and open, and his open marketplace would allow sellers to compete on a level playing field. Capitalism for the masses.

The moneymakers then were indeed the "big guys." They changed the webscape from burgeoning mom-and-pop e-commerce sites to mechanical credit card number suckers. No longer were sellers looking for customers; the customers were reduced to "eyeballs," "page views," and "wallets." Respect for those who visited the sites went down the drain, once they had been reduced to charts and numbers.

Rather than an oligarchy, where power was held by a few elite members, Pierre set out to make a community where buyers and sellers could converse, ask questions, and share ideas. He took the old Internet ideas to AuctionWeb and built community boards.

Around this time, the name of the site changed to eBay, and Pierre instituted the Web's first community feedback system. He wanted the site to be based on the moral code that he, himself, embraced. So early in 1996, Pierre posted this notice on the site:

Posted: February 26, 1996

I launched eBay's AuctionWeb on Labor Day, 1995. Since then, the site has become more popular than I ever expected, and I began to realize that this was indeed a grand experiment in Internet commerce. By creating an open market that encourages honest dealings, I hope to make it easier to conduct business with strangers over the net.

Most people are honest. And they mean well. Some people go out of their way to make things right. I've heard great stories about the honesty of people here. But some people are dishonest. Or deceptive. This is true here, in the newsgroups, in the classifieds, and right next door. It's a fact of life. But here, those people can't hide. We'll drive them away. Protect others from them. This grand hope depends on your active participation. Become a registered user. Use our feedback forum. Give praise where it is due; make complaints where appropriate. For the past six months, I've been developing this system single-handedly, in my spare time. Along the way, I've dealt with complaints among participants. But those complaints have amounted to only a handful. We've had close to 10,000 auctions since opening. And only a few dozen complaints. Now, we have an open forum. Use it. Make your complaints in the open. Better yet, give your praise in the open. Let everyone know what a joy it was to deal with someone. Above all, conduct yourself in a professional manner. Deal with others the way you would have them deal with you. Remember that you are usually dealing with individuals, just like yourself. Subject to making mistakes. Well-meaning, but wrong on occasion. That's just human. We can live with that. We can deal with that. We can still make deals with that. Thanks for participating. Good luck, and good business!

Regards,

Pierre Omidyar

With this notice, and the formation of the boards on the site, eBay became the first site to incorporate the type of community forum we now refer to as social media.

Today, the strategists and highly paid consultants would say that Pierre merely made his site "sticky," where users are compelled to hang around and browse the pages. The term *sticky* is today usually reserved for sites where there are many ads, which the site owner hopes will be noticed and clicked on. The only "ads" on the eBay site at the time were for the auctions, listing items for sale. It was truly an altruistic action, since there was no charge to the seller for posting or completing a sale.

By September of 1997, AuctionWeb, the little site that could, officially became eBay. Along with the name change came a new CEO, Margaret "Meg" Whitman, with an impressive background and plans to bring the site into the future. Buyers and sellers remained a community on the site, and the site rocketed to meteoric success. By 2000, eBay was worth more than Yahoo! and Amazon combined.

EBay changed e-commerce forever. By moving goods to those who valued them, the company became a social utility as well as an e-commerce site. Whatever changes have come and gone at

Figure 11.1   Pioneering eBay sellers ran their businesses via a community, and they are proud of it.

the site over the years, you can take my word for it, open forums still function for the users on eBay. I wrote about the open forums on my blog in 2009, under the title "Social Media Marketing? Learn from Successful eBay Sellers." Pierre saw my post and passed it along to his community on Twitter (see Figure 11.1).

When you consider how eBay changed the landscape of e-commerce, think about what the company accomplished, and how. Could opening up your site to customer participation help your sales? Perhaps just the addition of an interactive FAQ? Or customer reviews, to involve your customers with your products? Think about eBay: What magic did it instill?

Everything from A to Z, with a Smile: Amazon

Jeff Bezos was a Princeton graduate and young financial analyst. He ran a hedge fund for D. E. Shaw, a major Wall Street player, and became the firm's youngest senior vice president, in 1992.

While doing due diligence for the fund, Bezos was hit with a powerful reality: He realized that Internet usage was growing by 2,300 percent a year—a clear new investment opportunity.

In his already proven methodical fashion, Bezos studied the mail order business. Certainly, he believed, by studying the successful trends in retail and the leaders in mail order, he could come up with a sustainable business model. One of the advantages of selling via mail order was obvious: Sellers are normally not required to charge buyers sales tax, unless they have a presence in the customers' state (or *nexus*, as the Internal Revenue Service calls it).

Even though glossy catalogs were expensive to produce, the mail order business had been an American mainstay since 1893, when Sears, Roebuck & Co. began to sell rural America everything that could be found in big-city stores. (More on Sears in Chapter 13.)

Actually, it was Ben Franklin who started the mail order business, in 1774. And what did he sell? His backlog of unsold books. (I guess in those days very few books also became best sellers.) Even in the eighteenth century, Ben had his own slant on customer service. His catalogs proclaimed: "Those persons who live remote, by sending their orders and money to B. Franklin may depend on the same justice as if present."

Back in the twentieth century, Jeff Bezos made a list of 20 possible products to be sold on his site, then narrowed it to five: CDs, computer hardware, software, videos, and books. He found that the one commodity that wasn't widely sold through catalogs was books. Books were heavy and difficult to mail; but as a pure-play, it might be worked into a profitable business.

With books on the brain, Jeff flew to Los Angeles to attend the 1994 American Booksellers Association Convention, to learn everything he could about how to sell books. He learned that even in these early days of technology, book publishers and their wholesalers kept electronic inventories of every book published. He set up a Web site; the data entry was already taken care of.

Using a $300,000 investment from his parents' retirement fund to finance his endeavor, he set out to find programmers. Figure 11.2 shows an actual screenshot of the ad for future Amazon

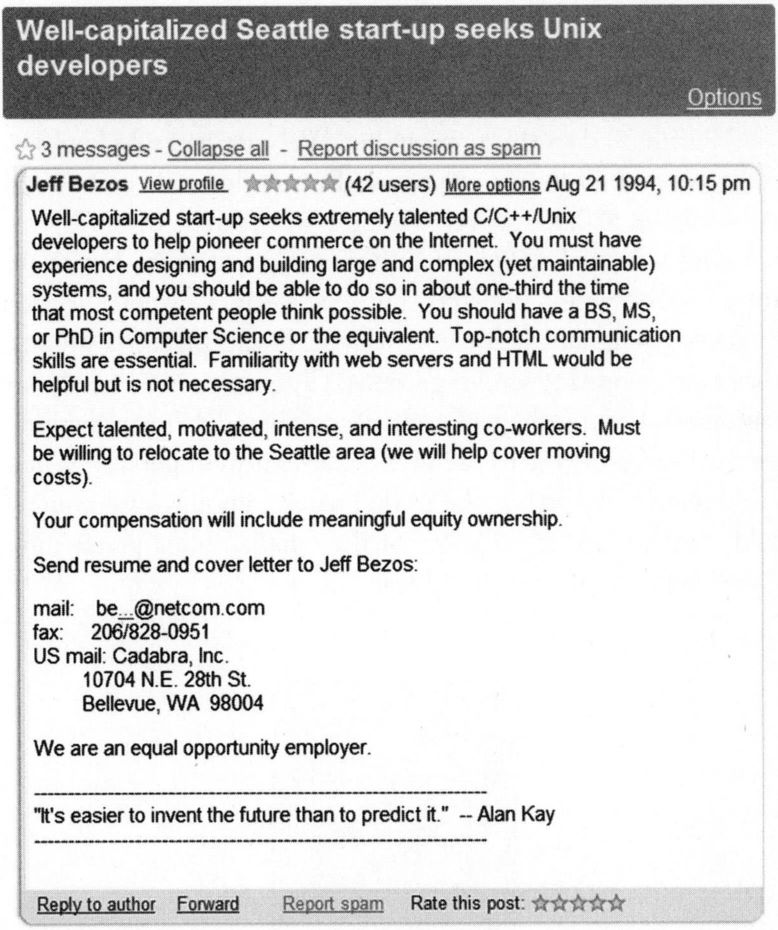

Well-capitalized Seattle start-up seeks Unix developers

Options

☆ 3 messages - Collapse all - Report discussion as spam

Jeff Bezos View profile ★★★★★ (42 users) More options Aug 21 1994, 10:15 pm

Well-capitalized start-up seeks extremely talented C/C++/Unix developers to help pioneer commerce on the Internet. You must have experience designing and building large and complex (yet maintainable) systems, and you should be able to do so in about one-third the time that most competent people think possible. You should have a BS, MS, or PhD in Computer Science or the equivalent. Top-notch communication skills are essential. Familiarity with web servers and HTML would be helpful but is not necessary.

Expect talented, motivated, intense, and interesting co-workers. Must be willing to relocate to the Seattle area (we will help cover moving costs).

Your compensation will include meaningful equity ownership.

Send resume and cover letter to Jeff Bezos:

mail: be...@netcom.com
fax: 206/828-0951
US mail: Cadabra, Inc.
        10704 N.E. 28th St.
        Bellevue, WA 98004

We are an equal opportunity employer.

"It's easier to invent the future than to predict it." -- Alan Kay
----

Reply to author   Forward   Report spam   Rate this post: ☆☆☆☆☆

Figure 11.2 Possibly the earliest ad for Amazon programmers, from 1994. Jeff Bezos knew exactly what he needed: top-notch communication skills.

programmers from Usenet groups. Note the Alan Kay quote at the bottom of the ad: "It's easier to invent the future than to predict it."

Invent the future he did. Jeff and his wife, Mackenzie, set up their new Web site in their two-bedroom home. The tables that held their three Sun microstations were made from doors bought at a hardware store. Once the code was set to go, he had friends and family test the system. They went live on July 1995 with the first Amazon logo, shown in Figure 11.3.

Within 30 days this unpromoted Web site had sold books in 50 states and 45 foreign countries. By September it had posted gross sales of $20,000 a week. Amazon went public in 1997.

Amazon has had its ups and downs since then, but those initial investments are worth millions today. Customer service has been paramount at Amazon from the beginning. Interestingly, the company used to send out logo-ed Christmas gifts to its regular customers. I received gifts for two years, then didn't get anything on the third year (I'm thinking this is after it went public). When I told them I felt bad because I didn't receive my gift, I was politely told they no longer did this; but they mailed me a pretty nifty Amazon puzzle magnet. It did make me smile.

Figure 11.3   Amazon's logo has gone through many changes since this first one.

Bezos, through his obsession with customer service, has made Amazon a consumer-centric organization. He's often quoted as saying, "If you build a great experience, customers tell each other about that. Word of mouth is very powerful." From the beginning he kept merchandise prices low, to strengthen long-term customer loyalty, and opened the site to customer reviews of products. The customer reviews built a community of readers who cared about books, the site, and each other. (Originally, reviews could be posted anonymously; now they must be attributed.)

Amazon is focused on its corporate culture. Bezos instituted the Just Do It program, which as in other successful companies, rewards employees who think outside the box and proceed with projects that benefit the company—without their boss's approval. In typical Bezos style, the physical "prize" was an old, used Nike shoe—reflecting the well-known Nike slogan. Employees valued that prize as a significant "atta boy."

When companies trust their employees to come up with great ideas, and allow them to follow through with them, it bodes well that they will have similar respect for the customer.

Similar to Pierre Omidyar's post to the eBay community, Bezos bases all his decisions on the Six Core Values he established for Amazon: customer obsession, ownership, bias for action, frugality, high hiring bar, and innovation. Maintaining these values stimulates focus on the company's operational strategies.

Bezos says, "We see our customers as invited guests to a party, and we are the hosts. It's our job every day to make every important aspect of the customer experience a little bit better."

Lots of companies spew corporate cultural platitudes, but where the rubber hits the road is with their employees. Bezos's respect for employee suggestions was revolutionary. By allowing innovation to come from the bottom, from the people closest to the problems, Amazon effectively addressed its most serious customer service issues.

Do you have a company meeting every week to listen to your employees? Might be a good idea. Also, be sure to keep the lines of communication open, and give your staff some leverage when it comes to making customers happy.

Changing the Way We Mail: Endicia

Ever think that your business is too brick-and-mortar to make it online? Perhaps consider a little innovation, a twist on your core product, so you can expand your customer base online. The Web is wide open to creative ideas.

Back in the day, I had to produce direct mail pieces for our clients. If you take a look at a return postcard, you'll see a lot of bar coding; the U.S. Postal Service (USPS) has stringent requirements as to the code's placement on the card. Meeting the requirements manually (i.e., with a ruler) made the USPS specifications a challenge. Without templates, mailing pieces were a real chore to design.

In the late 1990s, I attended COMDEX (the largest computer trade show in the world), where I came across a small booth with a couple of programmer-type guys. This was not terribly out of the ordinary, given the venue, but these two had a groundbreaking new software, called DAZzle. DAZzle was the very first WYSIWYG (what-you-see-is-what-you-get) mail-piece design tool in the industry. It was just a couple of guys with an idea: computers could generate postage for real-world mailing. The company, PSI Associates, had been founded by Dr. Harry Whitehouse (Harry, to all of his customers), in 1982, to develop software for address verification and mail management.

Harry also invented the online Dial-A-ZIP system. In 1991, his Personal Postage System prototype was presented at a USPS meeting in Washington, DC, during the brainstorming years of the USPS Information Based Indicia Program. Dial-A-ZIP became the first Internet-based address verification system, in 1996.

The company's crowning glory, the second-generation Internet-based version of the Personal Postage System, was invented in 1997; PSI was also awarded a patent for the Virtual Postage Meter that most of us use today (licensed by many companies selling Internet postage).

Harry went on to develop Endicia Internet Postage, in 2000, the first Internet postage service to offer Electronic Delivery Confirmation. It has been at the forefront of shipping technology ever since. Endicia was also the first, and remains the only, Internet postage service for Mac users.

That's not all. Have you seen those very cool stamps on which you can have your personal pictures? Well, Harry invented those, too, in 2005. This was about the time I did my PBS program, "Making Your Fortune Online," and to commemorate the event, Harry sent me my very own postage stamp featuring a shot from the show.

What Harry invented is what we know today as *online postage*. You'd probably guess that he spent a lot of time working with the companies that were transitioning to online postage services. That's an understatement. When it comes to his customers, no matter how small or large, Harry is there, offering help and guidance. He's always believed that the smallest customer may become the largest one day, so he gives respect and advice equally to all.

Harry instituted a help area on the Endicia site to ease the way for many of us in the field, called "Harry's Hints" (Figure 11.4). Giving these technical hints to early adopters and customers reflects the company's online commitment to customer service. Pretty much any question you may have on this technology is answered there.

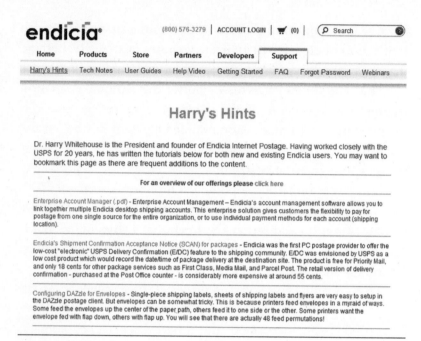

Figure 11.4   Harry's Hints is a staple among Endicia power users.

I went back to Google Groups (the historic Usenet again?) and found posts from Harry in forums, along with his personal help to users, dating continually since 2001. That's dedication—proof that he's still in the game even though Endicia was sold in 2007 to Newell Rubbermaid. A company name that goes beyond household goods, Newell Rubbermaid also owns many major pen brands, Liquid Paper, DYMO, CardScan, Mimio (the technology of writing on a whiteboard to projector), and more. It pretty much has the office technology market sewn up.

And as of this writing, all over the world, more than $4 billion in postage has been printed through Endicia—and Harry is still the CEO.

Which is why I was surprised when, as a customer of Endicia, I received a box of cookies from the company at Christmas. They were the best chocolate chip cookies I'd ever tasted and I scoured the packaging for a hint as to where they came from. There was no sign at all.

I e-mailed Harry and asked where the cookies came from. A couple of days later I got this reply: "I think you must be trying to butter me up, because I bake those cookies. I've baked them since I've been in college!"

You can take this story to mean one thing: If you allow yourself to stretch your imagination, the sky is the limit. Dream big, work hard, and don't give up—and never give up being a regular guy who actually "talks" to your customers.

LinkExchange Kick-Starts a Career

It was 1996, and two ex-Harvard roommates, Tony Hsieh and Sanjay Matan, were sitting around twiddling their thumbs (kinda sounds like the start of a bad bar joke, eh)? These guys were bored— you know, the kind of bored when you're willing to do just about anything? So to kill their boredom, they coded; that is, they spent their weekend writing computer code. By Monday, they had the shell for a new Web site. (Don't you wish *your* life was this easy?)

They had developed a Web site that enabled small online businesses to exchange advertising banners with each other. Wanting to beta-test their system, they reached out to 50 friends with sites. It worked so flawlessly that they opened it up to the public for business.

By 1998, the LinkExchange Banner Network, originally run out of Sanjay's apartment, was reaching over half of Internet-enabled households every month. By the time they had sold their home-brewed business to Microsoft, for $265 million, more than a million Web sites were exchanging banners over the network. They were reaching more households than Yahoo!

A business this successful doesn't happen overnight. The partners answered all e-mails themselves. When a customer e-mail would come in requesting service, they would drop everything and answer it. They often checked the e-mail box every 10 minutes. They wanted satisfied customers.

Tony had always been annoyed by lousy customer service. So the first employees that LinkExchange hired were customer service employees. The pair wanted to differentiate their company from the others in the field, and decided to do so by stressing the importance of customer retention and loyalty.

Not satisfied with the success of LinkExchange, Tony began investing in Internet startups. Wanting to get back in the game after the sale of LinkExchange, he joined Alfred Lin at Zappos (then an up-and-coming Web shoe retailer), as a part-time consultant. Alfred had worked with Tony as vice president of Finance and Administration at LinkExchange, and had managed the sale of the company. (Their relationship went way back, to college, when Tony was running a pizza business and Alfred was his number one customer.)

After a year doing part-time service at Zappos, Tony became a full-time staffer. His goal was to plan what the company wanted to stand for when it "grew up."

The goal of the company was to become a brand, not just about shoes, but a brand focused on good customer service. That way, it wouldn't be pigeonholed into just selling shoes. The plan was that, in 10 years, people wouldn't realize Zappos just sold shoes and it could expand.

The sky's the limit now. The Zappos brand now encompasses a wide variety of merchandise, from shoes to beauty items to housewares. Tony told me that the eventual goal for Zappos "is to be a number one brand based on customer service—perhaps someday even expanding into a Zappos airline."

Along with customer service, Tony believes in a positive corporate culture; it's his number one priority. The Zappos culture is reflected in its 10 core values:

1. Deliver Wow through Service
2. Embrace and Drive Change
3. Create Fun and a Little Weirdness
4. Be Adventurous, Creative, and Open-Minded
5. Pursue Growth and Learning
6. Build Open and Honest Relationships with Communication
7. Build a Positive Team and Family Spirit
8. Do More with Less
9. Be Passionate and Determined
10. Be Humble

Zappos wants its employees to believe in themselves and the customers, to think for themselves and do what it takes to succeed. Being humble is important, too.

Corporate culture imbues all Zappos employees. They are not just encouraged to embrace the corporate culture; it is a requirement of employment. Hiring an employee requires two sets of interviews, one to assess technical ability and one to determine culture fit.

The annual employee review is based 50 percent on performance and 50 percent on living up to core values. No matter how good employees are at their jobs at Zappos, they may lose their positions if the corporate values aren't paramount to them. As I discuss in Chapter 10, the employee environment goes a long way to promoting the zeitgeist of a company and the quality of customer service that it delivers.

All this attention to corporate culture and forward-thinking management allowed Zappos.com, in November 2008, to cross the $1 billion threshold in sales. Less than a year later it was sold to another customer-obsessed company, Amazon, for $1.2 billion. Tony remains as CEO and still works out of his cubicle, planning bigger and better things for the company. Alfred Lin, Tony's old pizza buddy, announced he would be leaving Zappos in January 2011, to become a venture capitalist with Sequoia.

The entrepreneurs described in this chapter started from scratch, and their quest for success was matched by their reverence for people—their customers and their employees. Customer service isn't just about giving customers what they want; it's all about respect.

12

Small-Business Examples

How They Did It Right

A large group of forward-thinking businesses and energetic entrepreneurs are working the online world to reach their customers. Many are successful in their endeavors, and others are not. What does it take to succeed with customers online? Can your business meet the challenge?

I have received a lot of feedback that while social media outreach is fine for big businesses, most small businesses seem to feel they don't have the staff to undertake such activities. It's true that social media may take some time, but a little organization on your part can turn this "task" into an enjoyable, profitable pastime.

Social media has made customer service the new marketing. There are many shining examples of smaller businesses that have successfully utilized social media to reach their customers. Savvy small businesses are making customers happy online, and you can too. The case studies in this chapter provide helpful examples that you can observe and pick up a few tips from. In the next chapter I'll describe an interesting group of big-business types that are reaching out to their customers online, tell you where to find them, and what you can learn from them.

Jason Falls (@JasonFalls), founder of the consulting company Social Media Explorer LLC (www.socialmediaexplorer.com) organizes online outreach for businesses of all sizes. He came up with the data shown in Table 12.1 on how three companies were staffing their Twitter customer service outreach in 2009.

The findings in the table show that businesses evaluate their online commitments in different ways. Since Twitter is largely populated by early adopters, and its audience is continually morphing, the decision as to how much staff to devote to customer service seems somewhat up in the air. One thing does stand out: A huge staff (in relation to total number of employees) is not

Table 12.1   Staffing Social Media Service

	Comcast	Network Solutions	United Linens
Number on staff	10	2	2
Hours/Day (per person)	8 (Twitter just one part of full community engagement efforts)	Less than 1	Less than 1
Special Staff/ Integrated	Digital Care Department	Social Media Team is own department	Marketing Department
Success Metrics	How we change the organization	Low negative online sentiment; number of people engaged; media placements	Relationships built for new business potential

From Jason Falls "Customer Twervice," Social Media Explorer LLC, 2009.

necessary. If larger companies can produce positive results in less than a couple of hours a day, imagine how the flexibility of your small business could work in your favor. Your efforts in connecting with your customers can only pay off in loyalty.

Properly serving your customers requires that you, first, listen to their needs and, second, respond quickly. Check out any related online profiles for quality engagement. Remember that numbers of followers or fans means very little unless you back up those numbers with some sort of collaborative interaction.

If you're a brick-and-mortar store or business that doesn't offer any kind of product/service exchange via the Web, you can still reach customers online. Having an e-presence doesn't mean you have to be engaged in e-commerce. While we rarely think of professional service providers as having to build their own businesses, there are many accountants, lawyers, doctors, and veterinarians who've done an amazing job of this online.

The Veterinarian

One example of a professional who has built an effective customer service and outreach platform online is Dr. Annmarie Hill, owner and main veterinarian of Animal Center of Huntington Beach, California. Dr. Hill has done a great job of building community by following people on Twitter. This local vet, who uses the handle @VetLovingPetsHB, has more than 8,000 followers that she engages on a regular basis. She talks about dogs and cats and a bit about her personal life, which makes her communications personable to all. Her biography on Twitter reads:

> Animal Care Center of Huntington Beach veterinarian serving Fountain Valley, Costa Mesa, Newport Beach, Orange County. www.acchb.com. #dogs #cats #animals #pets

Notice how she covers her location and her practice; and best of all, she hashtags her specialties. Her link to her business Web site brings up the page shown in Figure 12.1.

Once Dr. Hill draws people to her Web site, she offers a free first exam. The home page, rather than selling, immediately lets the viewer know who she is, and *gives* them a reason to do business with her. She also has links to recent articles and to her Facebook fan page (Figure 12.2)—another place where she's building her practice.

Dr. Hill is also testing the waters on other sites, including Foursquare, Gowalla and Whrrl—all of which she uses to offer special deals and discounts, as well as links to content. This generates excitement among her clients, and Dr. Hill finds it enjoyable

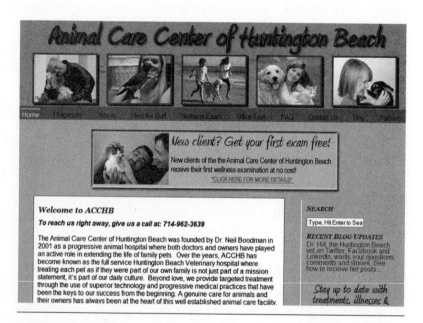

Figure 12.1   What could be more welcoming on a Web site than a free offer?

Figure 12.2 The Facebook page for the Animal Care Center of Huntington Beach is active with comments from clients and associates.

to interact with potential and current clients and build her business through this kind of social networking. Since she's become involved in her online customer service, she's seen a jump in her patient load.

Pet owners are generally a social group, who truly love their animals. (How many do you know who have pictures of their pets on their phones?) By integrating her personality with news about her clients and solid information on the needs of pet owners, Dr. Hill gives clients a reason to visit her sites—and her business.

Whatever your profession, you can easily emulate her example, no matter how mundane your business seems to you.

The Vineyard

Although many people tend to think of wineries as "big businesses," many family-owned vineyards are struggling—right along with the rest of us—to build their brands.

Social media director, author, and certified sommelier Rick Bakas works with the Skalli family, owners of the St. Supéry vineyards in Napa Valley, California. Rick's job is to help the Skallis connect with their customers on the Web. Now, you might be wondering, customer service for a winery? You're probably thinking that the best customer service is to offer wine tastings. Well, that's just what Rick does—online.

Figure 12.3 shows a picture of the St. Supéry Facebook fan page, used to build relations with more than 8,000 wine-loving fans. (Note the mention of the upcoming virtual wine tasting on Twitter.)

St. Supéry has been running virtual wine tastings for a few months now via online chats, where they announce a particular wine varietal and a calendar date. Participants then purchase their bottles for the tasting. Wines are tasted in real time on the prescribed day, and everyone posts their tasting notes online. The winery's Sauvignon Blanc tasting was particularly popular, drawing more than 650 contributors worldwide. Rick also gives tips and information on wine (plus a little personal data) on his own Twitter account @RickBakas, while the company tweets from its account, @StSupery.

Aside from its activity on Twitter and Facebook, St. Supéry has used Foursquare in a very clever way. It ran a promotion that rewards people who check in at restaurants and bars that serve the vineyard's wines and leave a "tip." Customers receive a point for

Figure 12.3 On Facebook, St. Supéry announces events and interacts with wine lovers worldwide.

every tip they leave at each check-in. The user e-mails a screen shot of the tip—along with his or her contact information—to the winery. Points can be accumulated over a specified length of time and cashed in as follows:

1 tip: St. Supéry Drop Stop

5 tips: Foil Cutter

7 tips: Purse Hook

15 tips: Logo Baseball Cap

20 tips: Logo Corkscrew

25 tips: Dollarhide Vineyard mouse pad

50 tips: Personal Skype tasting with winemaker Michael Scholz and/or Rick Bakas

Not only does this type of promotion build goodwill with patrons, but it helps the business create a mailing list for future promotions. St. Supéry's standard Foursquare promotion? When you check in at the Napa valley winery on Foursquare, you see a notice that says: "Show that you've checked in to St. Supéry on Foursquare to get a complimentary tasting for you and a guest." The best part of this tactic is that it generates a lot of customer support, because the person is already on location.

The entire staff at St. Supéry is reaching out and answering questions via the following Twitter feeds:

@StSuperyVC: Contact to employees at the tasting bar
@EmmaSwain: To follow the CEO of St. Supéry
@SkalliWines: To chat with the family that owns the winery
@mrwinemaker: To connect with the winemaker himself

The winery also uploads videos about winemaking and more to its account on YouTube, as shown in Figure 12.4.

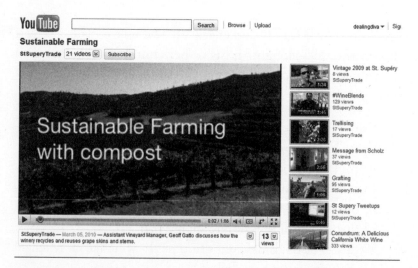

Figure 12.4   Videos make for interesting viewing for wine aficionados.

The Restaurant

There are a whole lot of people out there who are working really hard to connect with their customers via the Web. Even small restaurants are reaching out to their customers online. I spoke to Joe Sorge, whose family owns five Milwaukee restaurants, including one called Water Buffalo (@water_buffalo). Joe works hard to keep up with his online customer service, and enjoys the immediacy with which he can deliver it from Twitter. He told me that participating in social media permits him to apply the same customer service style that his family employs in their restaurants, only in an online format.

If Joe sees a negative comment appear in the Twitter stream, he immediately grabs the tweet and texts it to his management on site. This helps to resolve the problem before it becomes a larger issue. Joe responds publicly to the comment as well, which affords him the benefit of showing his customers that the restaurant truly does care about its customers enough to address their issues in a timely manner.

The @AJBombers Twitter background, designed for another one of Joe's restaurants, reflects the value Joe places on his customers (see a segment of the page in Figure 12.5). Every year, Joe holds a holiday tweetup at the restaurant. Last year he pulled out a large piece of vellum and had everyone in attendance sign it. He then set this as the background on his page to show that his customers are of utmost importance to him.

Joe's blog, theburgerwhisperer.com, features photos and reviews of customer-created burgers he has served at his restaurant. Joe also avidly participates on other sites, such as Yelp, Facebook, and Foursquare. He gives a free burger for dethroning the current mayor and a free cookie for adding a tip or a "to-do" on Foursquare.

Figure 12.5 AJ Bombers' Twitter background clearly states that customers are number one.

I spoke to Joe about the part community plays in the restaurant business, and he said, "The hospitality industry has always been dependent on community. Online social media provides a magnifying glass . . . it [amplifies] the importance of . . . community, [emphasizes the] deep need [people have] to belong."

When new customers come into Joe's restaurant and meet him, many say that they feel like they already know him from his online outreach. *That's* the power of online service engagement.

Food Trucks

Though in the past referred to as "roach coaches," food trucks are no longer déclassé, and they seem to be popping up everywhere now. People from all walks of life are chasing down their favorite foods from a wide variety of vendors-on-wheels offering gourmet—and not so gourmet—cuisine. Since a food truck's audience is typically limited by geography, people tend to discover them either by word of mouth or, increasingly, via a Twitter search. By announcing their locations and specials on their Web sites and Twitter and Facebook accounts, many of these trucks have built a large customer base.

This is the clearest example of how being present, and communicating via social media, can expand the reach of a business beyond what a Web site alone can do. Although there's not a lot of interaction on these accounts, letting customers know where they are, what hours they will be there, as well as what is being served, is a great way to manage customer expectations. And letting customers know when the truck will be in a different location *before* they head out for lunch helps ensure their return when the truck comes back to their neighborhood. If these vendors would "shout out" to their customers, chances are that their businesses would grow even faster.

Though I live in a big city where trends are quick to emerge and take hold, food trucks are getting popular all over the country. There are a huge number here in Los Angeles from which to choose. Most are on Facebook and have their own Web sites; here are just a few, with their Twitter IDs.

@KogiBBQ: Korean barbeque
@COOLHAUS: Custom ice cream sandwiches
@nomnomtruck: Banh Mi food
@grlldcheesetruk: Grilled-cheese sandwiches
@buttermilktruck: Gourmet pancakes
@LoukstoGo: Greek food
@BabysBBS: Burgers

Think of the opportunities that communicating via social media opens for those with a creative mind and a good product. A good example is the new creative twist at @Worldfare, the world's first double-decker "bustaurant," with "a chef down below and a party on top!"

Mobile Computer Repair

I recently came across a funny guy on Twitter who operates under the handle @EricGreenspan. I soon learned that he's a very active member of the online community and owns a company called Make It Work. Even as the head of the company, Eric is out in the world, building the brand and talking to real people. His company is also on Twitter under @MakeItWork—although his personal account seems to be the best promotion for his business.

Make It Work, which offers mobile technology support, claims to be able to repair anything that "hums, beeps, or clicks." The techs drive red logo-ed MINI Coopers to customer's homes and offices—usually after they've reached the end of their rope with their computers—and have a reputation for providing excellent customer service. The Make It Work Web site features a page of testimonials from its customers—30,000 and counting.

When I asked Eric about Make It Work, he said that customer service is his number-one goal; he wants every customer to be "delighted." In fact, Eric refers to himself as a "customer service activist"—and that's why he wants to make sure that he and his company are out there for all to see.

Of course the company has a Facebook page, Twitter account, and company blog, but the best part is Eric's personal blog, where he occasionally posts some very personal reflections. Take a look in Figure 12.6 at the way he uses it to promote his business in a very nonpromotional way.

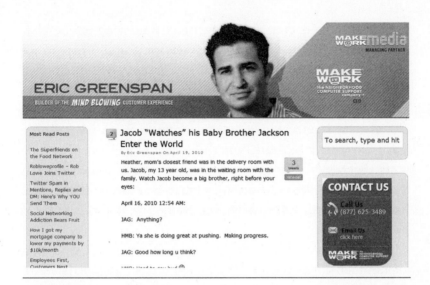

Figure 12.6 Eric shares a special moment—the birth of his son—with customers on his blog.

This post covers birth of his son right alongside discussions about his company. Mixing personal posts along with professional topics not only reveals your personal side, but adds a little tabloid-type pizzazz. Transparency is what this is all about, and Eric does a great job.

Linen Supply

United Linen & Uniform Services (@UnitedLinen) is a perfect example that it's not all about numbers in your audience. You might assume that a small business-to-business company established in 1936 and located in Bartlesville, Oklahoma, might not be on top of the latest customer service trends. But this company, which started as a personal laundry service with home pickup and delivery, is now a major player in online customer service.

Marketing director Scott Townsend is utilizing online platforms to handle countless customer service issues. When an ice storm paralyzed his company's area last winter, the staff notified customers about the status of the deliveries through Twitter, in addition to announcing it on the company Web site and making phone calls. United Linen also maintains a Facebook fan page and a blog that is separate from the company Web site. The blog posts about local events, as well as innovations and changes in the industry. Videos on various subjects are also posted to sites like DailyMotion, Yahoo, MySpace, MetaCafe, Blip.tv, and i2TV by using TubeMogul.

The company is fairly famous for its instructional videos on napkin folding (see Figure 12.7), a topic that's very germane to the business. Scott claims that if you laid all the napkins the company launders in a single day end to end, they would stretch for 24 miles! United Linen's active YouTube channel is filled with

Figure 12.7   Smart promotion shares space with conversation on United Linen's Twitter stream.

posts of videos to introduce new employees, show "how it's done" to customers, and give insider views of the company.

You've seen some good illustrations here of small businesses that are doing a good job of online customer outreach. Now check out the Web sites, Facebook pages, and Twitter feeds of these companies for ideas on how you, too, can better serve your customers online.

13

Lessons from Big Business
Leaders in Customer Service

Not everyone wants to be, or even *can* be, big business. But big business has a lot more money to spend trying out new things. One of the ways small businesses can improve their customer service and overall bottom line is to study the latest things that big guys are doing.

Larger organizations often have to observe a fair number of restrictions when establishing and carrying out their social media customer service outreach programs. They often have several layers of management that have to approve such plans, as well. Small business can be more flexible. You can conduct community outreach on a far smaller scale without having to staff a department.

Manish Mehta, vice president of Social Media and Community at Dell Inc., conveyed an interesting observation of small-business methods in a *Huffington Post* blog:

> "Mom and Pop" knew that their business was only as successful as their relationships with customers could make it. That's the value of the direct connection to your customer, and that's how every company can achieve success using social media—by facilitating the conversation. No strategy necessary.

This chapter will reveal some multimillion-dollar examples of what big business is doing in customer service, and how those strategies can be scaled for your small business. These companies have been around the block, and are really putting forth effort not only to reach, but also serve, their customers online.

Take a look at what they're doing, then consider whether they are actually doing it right. What would you do to improve their methods? Consider how you might apply what you learn here to your own business.

These companies are popping up on Facebook, Flickr, LinkedIn, YouTube, and Twitter more and more often. It would be nice if you could cover all those bases, as well (don't forget Foursquare and Yelp—very important to small biz), but it's okay if you can't. The most important thing is to do what you can to pay more online attention to your customer.

Consumers are learning to follow the companies they do business with on Twitter and Facebook *when* they are given a return on their time investment. Many prefer the immediacy that Twitter offers in the case of a customer service issue, since most companies tend to respond quickly there—perhaps because their reactions take place on such a public forum. Twitter's stream also is tracked by Google, and much of what is tweeted also appears as part of Google searches.

Customers expect good service and prompt resolution to problems. A winning customer service formula is practiced by companies that dedicate themselves to monitoring mentions and intervening with customer issues online. Responding appropriately and swiftly develops trust.

Online interaction, being a community activity, leads to many people jumping in to solve a problem; and when companies come to the fore, they score in their public perception. A company that chimes in to respond to customer issues prevents the online buzz that otherwise might escalate into large-scale customer concerns.

As described in Chapter 8 on the generations, people differ in how they like to reach out and be reached. Many aren't comfortable when they are asked to follow or friend others online. But when they reach out for help with an issue, they increasingly expect a brand to jump to the fore and intervene. Being transparent and authentic in voice, through social media outreach, leads to trust and loyalty.

Many big companies that are on Twitter have a team of people whose sole responsibility is to respond to tweets about them. Each person "signs" his or her tweets with his or her initials to personalize the outreach. Not a bad idea if you have more than one person sending tweets from your account.

Here are examples of some of the companies that are doing extraordinary online customer service work.

Comcast

Frank Eliason, as senior director of National Customer Service Operations for Comcast, was legendary on Twitter as the original

@ComcastCares. He's been written up in major media—from the blog "TechCrunch" to the *Wall Street Journal*—as the man who brought customer service to Twitter.

Frank has been revolutionary in his attempts to change the way we think about cable service providers—and online customer service. As an industry, this group has traditionally had a difficult time delivering quality customer service. Even though cable service companies often experience interruptions, equipment failures, and outages, it is rare to find someone at these companies to whom customers can vent their frustration.

At Comcast, Frank was that person; as @ComcastCares, he was out there listening for things that didn't go as planned. Looking at his stream, you'll frequently see the rapid-fire replies he posted to customer complaints and queries—as often as every few minutes. He tweeted from the Web, Twitterific, and often from his phone through SimplyTweet. As you can see in Figure 13.1, a screenshot of five minutes of his @ComcastCares stream, he's got great energy.

At Comcast, Frank went above and beyond to personalize himself to customers. He listed his family Web site and his blog on his Twitter page. He put himself out there, and put forth Herculean efforts to solve an almost neverending barrage of customer issues.

Frank left Comcast in 2010 to join Citi as senior vice president of social media. Whether Frank's replacement at @ComcastCares, Bill Gerth, and his crew can change the image of cable companies is still unknown; however, what they can do (and are doing) is working hard to solve customer problems as quickly as possible.

Although at one point he was the only individual at @ComcastCares, Bill now gets help from other Twitter accounts in the Comcast customer service department, such as @Comcast

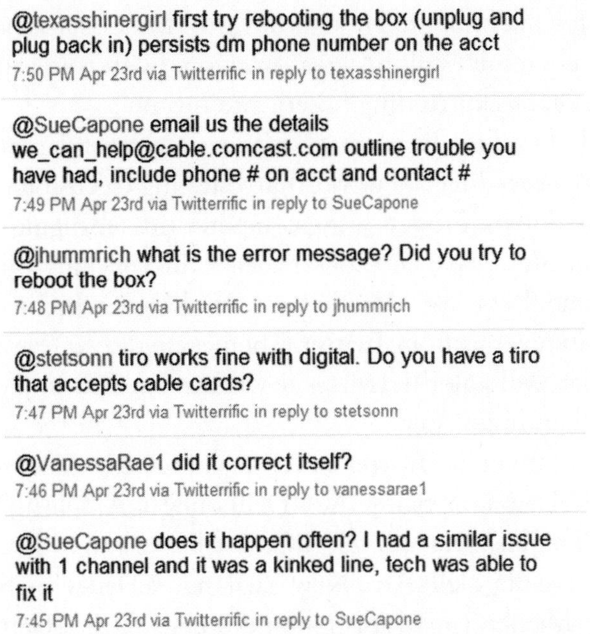

@texasshinergirl first try rebooting the box (unplug and plug back in) persists dm phone number on the acct
7:50 PM Apr 23rd via Twitterrific in reply to texasshinergirl

@SueCapone email us the details we_can_help@cable.comcast.com outline trouble you have had, include phone # on acct and contact #
7:49 PM Apr 23rd via Twitterrific in reply to SueCapone

@jhummrich what is the error message? Did you try to reboot the box?
7:48 PM Apr 23rd via Twitterrific in reply to jhummrich

@stetsonn tiro works fine with digital. Do you have a tiro that accepts cable cards?
7:47 PM Apr 23rd via Twitterrific in reply to stetsonn

@VanessaRae1 did it correct itself?
7:46 PM Apr 23rd via Twitterrific in reply to vanessarae1

@SueCapone does it happen often? I had a similar issue with 1 channel and it was a kinked line, tech was able to fix it
7:45 PM Apr 23rd via Twitterrific in reply to SueCapone

Figure 13.1 While at Comcast Frank (now @FrankEliason) on Twitter) was known for his rapid-fire tweets.

Bill, @ComcastBonnie, @ComcastDete, @ComcastMelissa, and @ComcastSteve. Making this a collaborative effort is certainly a step in the right direction, taking into account the large number of Comcast subscribers. The team shares their feedback via a newsletter to the bigwigs at Comcast every day. While it remains unclear whether the team can make Comcast number one in customer service, their efforts have certainly netted the company millions of dollars in positive ink.

Dell

Dell's senior manager of Corporate Affairs, Richard Binhammer— also known as @RichardatDell—has a bit more of a social than corporate tweet stream. He's known worldwide as a social media expert, as a result of all his great work on Twitter, and since Dell became famous for turning tweets into revenue.

Dell's social media outreach first became legendary when the company proved to the world that listening to customers could turn into dollars. From posting computer tips, engaging in social chat, and offering bargain coupon deals, the company announced in the middle of last year that its @DellOutlet had earned $3 million in revenue from Twitter. Then came the 2009 announcement that Dell's global Twitter reach had resulted in more than $6.5 million in revenue.

There are now Twitter accounts in Brazil, @DellnoBrasil; Canada @DellHomeSalesCA, @DellLoungeCA, @DellDomicile CA (in French); Ireland, @DellOutletIE; Australia @DellHome SalesAU, @Biz_Dell_AU; New Zealand, @DellHomeSalesNZ; @@Dell_Mexico (in Spanish)—and dozens more. (Dell lists all their current Twitter accounts on a corporate Web page: www.dell .com/Twitter). Some of those accounts deal solely with customer service, while others sell. This seems to beg the question: Is Dell's outreach focused on customer service, public relations, or sales? In a recent interview with *AdWeek*, Richard Binhammer claimed that the underlying goal behind *everything* they do at Dell it to reach consumers.

Dell's outreach on Facebook has been just as important to the company. It recently made donations to plant trees on behalf of its Facebook fans in honor of Earth Day (see Figure 13.2). This was just one element of the company's green program, meant to promote its efforts in recycling, bamboo packaging, and production of energy-efficient products. All fans had to do was "like" Dell on their Facebook pages and a donation would be made. The company ended up planting a total of about 6,500 trees.

An additional return on the investment for Dell was the discovery that listening to customers in real time helps the team

Plant
a tree for a friend.

Help us build a healthier planet, one tree at a time. **Dell is making a donation to The Conservation Fund to plant up to 150,000 trees on behalf of our Facebook fans.** It's easy to join in: **Become a fan, pick a friend and Dell will plant one of these trees on behalf of them.**

Click the "become a fan" or the "like" button at the top to get started.

Figure 13.2 A simple message from Dell netted thousands of donations.

uncover issues with new products as they release, enabling the company to develop new drivers almost immediately, to prevent future problems.

DISH Network

Cable and dish companies undoubtedly get a seemingly disproportionate number of complaints from their customers; they are, after all, in an industry where online service can be pretty dicey. I personally have DISH Network service in my house, so when I had a question, I searched online. I found the company on Twitter, tweeted a question, and got a speedy response.

DISH Network follows back its fans on Twitter, and dishes out (get it?) *actual* help, rather than reciting the usual corporate rah-rah. Based on the answers the customer service reps provide to their customers, they really seem to care about the issues at hand; and the company's stream is peppered with special deals and freebies when available.

I've seen them do everything from check appointment times, give box reset instructions, and diagnose picture issues. It seems they also monitor current DISH Network mentions (see Figure 13.3). When they see one, they will send a reply "Official DISH feed here, caught your tweet! Let us know if you'd like some help." Nice that they do an end-run around possible negative situations. Nipping problems in the bud is what online customer service is all about.

Customers will also find a very intuitive troubleshooting area on the DISH Network Web site. There's a Frequently Asked Questions page and an AskDISH interactive support tool. Should a customer not find at the site what he or she needs help with, there's also Live Chat.

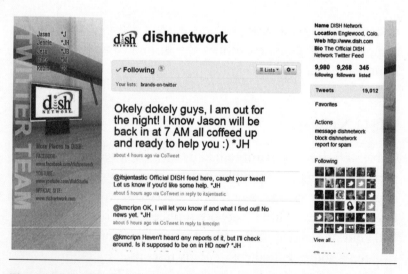

Figure 13.3   DISH Network even helps its followers find their remotes!

In its 2010 report, the American Customer Satisfaction Index (ACSI), a national economic indicator of customer evaluations of the quality of products and services available to household consumers in the United States, DISH Network was rated the leader among satellite and cable providers. It scored 71 in customer satisfaction—a significant seven-point increase from 2009. That sizeable jump partly reflects the company's forays into online customer service.

"DISH Network's dramatically improved ranking in the ACSI survey is testimony to the considerable strides we made over the past year to reestablish our leadership in customer service," said Charlie Ergen, chairman, president, and CEO of DISH Network. "We know our customers have many choices when it comes to TV," he continued, "which is why we remain committed to providing them with best-in-class service at an unmatched value."

DISH currently rotates Twitter replies from five members of its team. It's interesting that the company follows back everyone who follows them. I asked Robin, head tweetmeister for DISH, about this policy. She had words that rang true for me, and I hope for you as well:

> The reason we use Twitter as a brand is to engage with consumers, specifically with DISH Network customers. What type of connection would we be creating if we didn't afford them the opportunity to speak to us one-on-one when they'd prefer? If a Twitter user feels our updates are relevant enough to appear on his/her homepage, the least we can do as a company is return the favor and open the direct line of private communication with that person, as opposed to forcing him/her to address us publicly through an @ mention each time he/she has a question. When you get down to it, it's about

reciprocating the respect our followers have extended our way with their decision to follow @dishnetwork.

You can also find DISH Network on Facebook, YouTube, and of course, its own corporate site.

Domino Sugar

Check out the @DominoSugar Twitter feed and Facebook pages. This venerable old company is dishing out old-fashioned customer service via the most modern methods available. Its chatty stream engages with cooking fans, solves baking problems, promotes bake sales, and gives out recipes.

For its customers who have a passion for baking, www.domino sugar.com offers unique ideas, resources, and support. Domino turns customer service into a science by providing recipes, downloadable calendars, measurement charts, party ideas, printable baking gift tags, and more. The company also gets behind nationwide charities, in the form of donations and promotions. Site visitors can also join Domino's virtual baking community to share and get the latest tips from other customers.

On its very active Facebook page, it reads, "For over 100 years, Domino® Sugar has been supplying the key ingredient that helps bakers everywhere show their families just how much they care." Domino knows its customers. It has heavy interaction with its fans, and follows them back, so they can be contacted through direct messages.

General Motors

Connie Burke is the person behind General Motors' online outreach. Connie has been with GM for over 25 years, and

Figure 13.4   The GM Customer Service team gets social with their customers.

is now working under the title of communications manager (North Central Region). It's apparent when talking to her or tweeting her personal account (@ConnieBurke) that she is not just an employee, but a fan of the product, as well. Launched in November 2009, the GM customer service Twitter account (@GMCustomerSvc) is managed by four GM customer service agents, who respond to issues of any kind, as you can see in Figure 13.4.

According to Connie, the @GMCustomerService account

> has been a significant differentiator with respect to our relationships with our customers. Our customers are everything; without them, we have no reason for being. This is

one example of how GM is trying new and effective ways to engage and retain our customer base. From General Motors' standpoint, our social media outreach efforts are not just another public relations program. We are interested in keeping the relationship going. Once you are family, we want to keep you in the family.

She told me a great story about GM's Twitter customer outreach: "We had a customer tweet that he had to take his Silverado to the dealership with a transmission concern for the second time in less than 2,000 miles. He was concerned this may become a recurring problem." GM responded to his tweet and advised him that his concern was covered under the 5-year/100,000-mile Powertrain warranty, and offered him a year of free maintenance for his inconvenience. By monitoring tweets, the social media team turned a potentially unhappy customer into a happy one— for the entire online world to see.

The company currently has 11 Twitter accounts (you can search for your specific car brand), @GMblogs, and six Facebook pages, where the team communicates with customers all over the country. The individual General Motors brand Web sites have thorough help sections; Cadillac even has an online chat area to service its owners. The brand sites also have communities called "Owners Centers" for the individual brands at www.gm.com /gmownercenter, hosted by Yahoo.com.

Ford Motor Company

The head of social media at Ford is the engaging Scott Monty (@ScottMonty). Scott has his own lively Twitter stream, as well as an excellent blog where he offers social media advice and views. Most of Scott's outreach is in the form of @ replies, and he's heavily involved in online conversation. He currently has about 45,000 followers—and he follows back many.

Scott's response to the recent uncertain times in the automotive market was to launch the Fiesta Movement, a campaign that gave out 100 international models of the Ford Fiesta to people across the country, to get impressions, publicity, and feedback for the Ford Fiesta 18 months prior to its U.S. release. The videos alone from these 100 people have gotten more than 7 million views on YouTube.

Fiesta Movement 2 features preproduction fiestas in 16 localized markets, through social media leader teams (see Figure 13.5). The Web site, www.fiestamovement2.com, features the teams and their stories. This is clearly *fantastic* marketing.

Scott has customer service covered, as well. For questions on any Ford product, check out @FordCustService on Twitter. It's

Figure 13.5 The Fiesta Movement blog has been a popular online destination.

run by Ford's customer service center, where reps are on duty from 8:00 AM to 5:00 PM (EST).

Scott has his own personal blog, too, at www.scottmonty .com; his 2010 New Year's post listed his social media predictions for the new year. One caught my attention (emphasis his): "Customers insist on custoMEr service. Check. More interaction on Facebook pages, Twitter, Get Satisfaction, and similar sites has customers looking for solutions wherever they can find it, not just via 800 numbers."

Ford maintains many other profiles on Twitter: @Ford, @Ford Fiesta, @FordAutoShows, @FordLatino, @FordEU, @FordAPA, and more. The list of employees who tweet at Ford can be found at http://twitter.com/ScottMonty/ford.

Finally, Ford maintains a single social media aggregation site, www.thefordstory.com, where everything online is brought together.

JetBlue

Airline JetBlue's Twitter account (@JetBlue) is perhaps one of the cheeriest, most helpful tweet streams. The voice of the account is Morgan Johnston, manager of Corporate Communications. @JetBlue sends out travel tips and helps customers when there's an issue that needs attention.

It's nice to see an airline that helps stranded passengers or potential customers with travel questions. Although its stream is very corporate oriented, JetBlue does a fine job of personalizing its messages to fans and customers. The "on-duty" JetBlue Twitter staff also has personal accounts, which you can find at www.twitter.com/JetBlue/team.

Morgan pointed out a shining example of JetBlue's customer outreach, a tribute to JetBlue's online customer service, as told by blogger Dave Raffaele. In his blog Dave talks about how, once, after deplaning from a flight, on which the thermostat of the plane may have malfunctioned, he tweeted: "@JetBlue: You need to turn down the heat on your 7:55 flight from Boston to Denver. It was rough."

Within a couple of minutes, JetBlue acknowledged Dave's concerns. Dave was impressed that he didn't receive an automated response, that there was a real person behind the brand. He said, "The fact that they had someone answer my comment makes me have faith that they did something about it."

On his return flight, he arrived at the airport early and found no one at the counter to check in his bag. He publicly tweeted his situation. Once again, JetBlue quickly acknowledged his comment and told him they were contacting a ground crew member to man the counter so he could check in his bag.

Later, Dave commented on his blog, "Ultimately, not being at the counter was not out of the norm for that red-eye [flight], but it was good to have someone on Twitter (both JetBlue and other folks) to give me the 411. A little information can go a long way to keeping customers happy, [and] that is what happened in this case."

This story provides real insight into just how closely JetBlue employees follow mentions of their company on social media sites—and proves that they're listening. They're also accomplishing their goal of engaging, by responding so swiftly to what they see, read, and hear.

JetBlue proclaims its Customer Bill of Rights on its Web site, at www.jetblue.com/about/ourcompany/promise/index.html. The airline's public pledge to its customers is admirable—as is the fact that it openly offers credits for breaches in service. The site has an easily accessible help page; and customers from most countries can reach JetBlue by phone from toll-free numbers.

You can follow the account, @jetbluecheeps, for deals on last-minute flights. They're posted to Twitter every Tuesday.

Kodak

Kodak's chief blogger and voice of @KodakCB is Jennifer Cisney. Not only will you find her on Twitter, but she also manages Kodak's corporate blog. Jennifer combines the Kodak brand logo with her personal picture to create an avatar that blends her corporate and personal identities. But it was Kodak's previous chief marketing officer (now author), Jeffrey Hayzlett (@JeffreyHayzlett), who started Kodak's online customer reach.

Kodak's marketing strategy embraces social media readily. Jeffrey has been known to talk about the "return on ignoring," rather than return on investment. He claims that, "If you're not engaged, then you're missing out. Conversations are going on with or without you. It used to be about eyes and ears; now you need to have hearts and minds."

In an interview, Jeffrey spoke about Kodak's outreach:

You want to engage, educate, excite people, and they become evangelists—or Kodak ambassadors is what we call them. That's what we call the "4 Es" So, it's very important for businesses or individuals, but especially for businesses, to get out there and engage with their communities.

Engaging is exactly what Kodak does, through various Twitter accounts, each of which covers a different aspect of the company's products and services: @GalleryExposure, @KodakConnect, @Kodak Printers, @KodakCommunity and @KodakEvents. And customers who are looking for bargains can check out @KodakDeals.

Kodak is doing more brand building than customer service through its social media platforms: evangelizing with a page on

Facebook, videos on YouTube and Flickr, free podcasts on iTunes, and four blogs. But the most important point is that they're listening.

You can find links to all of Kodak's social media activity at www.kodak.com/go/followus.

National Aeronautics and Space Administration (NASA)

Technology, the Internet, and space just seem to go together—right? So it's no surprise that NASA has jumped into social networking in a big way. NASA isn't big business, per se, but it is an organization with an important story to tell—one with a message the agency wants to get to as many people as possible. Perhaps the goal is to educate—or perhaps just to help us remember how fascinating all that space stuff truly is. Whatever the goal, you will find NASA at every turn in the social media landscape.

NASA started its online outreach program on Facebook and YouTube, followed by its first foray on Twitter in early May 2008, via the @MarsPhoenix account. This was the brainchild of Veronica McGregor, former CNN correspondent turned NASA news service manager at the Jet Propulsion Laboratory (JPL). Originally intending to use the Twitter account through landing day of the Mars Phoenix robotic spacecraft, and a couple of days after, the response from the online world was so overwhelming the decision was made to keep it going.

In an interview with the *Guardian*, McGregor said, "The followers seemed to appreciate having a source from inside a NASA mission who could give them news and information and answer questions. It was also helpful to be a bit playful on some of the posts, and I suppose that is how the personality developed."

Personality? For a space robot? @MarsPhoenix definitely has a personality of its own—commenting, tweeting pictures, replying to followers, and holding interviews with the press—"I know it *looks* easy, but you try following instructions sent from 182 million miles away!"

When the landing was imminent, @MarsPhoenix sent out a series of short tweets:

"parachute must open next. my signal still getting to Earth which is AWESOME!"
"parachute opening is scariest part for the team."
"parachute is open!!!!!"
"come on rocketssssss!!!!!"
"I've landed!!!!!!!!!!!!!"
"Cheers! Tears!! I'm here!"

The last tweet from @MarsPhoenix, posted on May 24, 2010, is shown in Figure 13.6.

The NASA accounts are some of the most popular online because of their quality content and interactivity between them

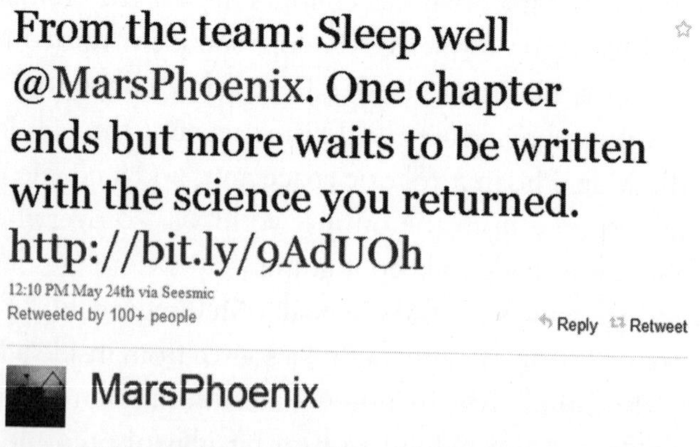

From the team: Sleep well @MarsPhoenix. One chapter ends but more waits to be written with the science you returned. http://bit.ly/9AdUOh

12:10 PM May 24th via Seesmic
Retweeted by 100+ people

Reply Retweet

 MarsPhoenix

Figure 13.6 This post from @MarsPhoenix no longer appears in the stream. NASA has resurrected the stream with news of Mars.

and their followers. If you visit www.nasa.gov/connect, you'll find links to over 55 official Twitter accounts, 35 Facebook pages, 21 YouTube channels, plus multiple sites on Flickr, Ustream, and MySpace. If you go to the list twitter.com/NASA/astronauts-in-space-now, you'll be able to follow the live tweet streams from space; you can also find the astronauts' personal tweets at twitter .com/NASA/astronauts. (The first astronaut to tweet from space was from Mike Massimino, @Astro_Mike, in early April 2009.)

NASA got smart about using social media, reaching out in a new way. The group posts updates for various NASA projects, research, and other activities, such as feeds about various telescopes and the space modules the agency has deployed.

To further extend its reach into the social media community, NASA holds tweetups (in-person meetings with Twitter followers) at its facilities. These are more than simple lectures; the online community is given the opportunity to go behind the scenes. Followers are able to speak with scientists, engineers, astronauts, and NASA managers. The agency's tweetups can be two hours or two days, depending on the event. (If you're interested, registration for NASA tweetups is announced on @NASA and @NASATweetup.) Pretty smart—but then again, they are rocket scientists.

Network Solutions

Network Solutions originally was solely a domain name registry; it now also offers Web hosting and full online marketing services. My first Web site, in 1996, was registered with the company because, at the time, there wasn't a lot of choice. It was the first domain name registry operating under a subcontract with the U.S. Defense Information Systems Agency (DISA), in 1991. In 1992, it was the sole bidder to further develop a domain name registry for the Internet, under a grant from the National Science Foundation (NSF). By 1993, Network Solutions was the sole name registrar for the .com, .net, and .org domains. The company didn't charge for registrations until 1996; and it wasn't 1999 that it had any competition.

This is obviously a forward-thinking company, so I wasn't surprised to see it become involved in social media. I first learned about this organization's online connection when I complained about a domain vendor I had tried on the Internet. I was directed to the @NetSolCares account, which is where I met Shashi Bellamkonda (@shashib), Network Solution's proclaimed "social media swami."

Network Solutions faced some challenges a few years ago when its customer satisfaction ratings went way down. Since then, by using online platforms, it has been able to build a much happier and more loyal customer base. Shashi happily told me, "Customers can get answers in one single tweet. There are no e-mails to open or respond to. We can [answer their questions] by just tweeting a link to our online resources—or turn the issue over to a representative."

Almost every tweet in Network Solution's stream is devoted to helping customers. In an industry where customers often have challenges and questions, Network Solutions is acknowledging—and solving—customers' problems online, right alongside them. Its Web site features a robust help center, www.networksolutions .com/support, which answers almost any question a customer might have. If further issues arise, customers can access representatives via a toll-free number or e-mail.

Customers who stay with Network Solutions are rewarded with Gold VIP status, after they've spent a total of $1,500 with the company. Once they're part of the loyalty program, they receive special membership program offers and exclusive pricing on many products and services. They also get a special Gold VIP phone line, which allows them to immediately speak to Gold VIP Customer Service Representatives—24/7.

Network Solutions has come a long way in bringing quality service to a service-starved industry.

Sears

When I was a kid, our family would go to Sears to buy appliances. As far as I knew, there was no other store that sold refrigerators. My mother trusted the Sears repairman and treated his words as gospel. I don't know what the store was doing in those days, but its customers were believers.

As many people know, the Sears shopping experience has suffered over the years. However, the company has been working hard to improve things, and shopping at Sears.com nowadays is a real pleasure (see Figure 13.7). After conducting a simple search for refrigerators on the site, I was shocked to see that there were 920 different options available. On the same page where items were listed, there was also a list of brands, sorted by customer ratings. A visit to the product page showed actual customer reviews, pros and cons about each item, and discussions that had ensued about particular items within the Sears online community.

This is where Sears has brought innovation to the Web. Approximately two million people a month visit MySears.com, a highly lauded community site that encourages customers to share their insights, experiences, and product reviews by creating a two-way dialogue between the retailers and purchasers, through discussion forums, blog entries, ratings, reviews, polls and surveys, and a comments platform.

I spoke to Robert Harles, Sears' vice president of Social Media and Community, about the site. When he joined Sears,

Figure 13.7   The MySears.com community continues to grow.

late in 2007, he said there was a sense that "we as a company may have lost track of who our customers were." Harles discussed our nation's transformation from one of local shopkeepers to major corporations. His goal is to return Sears to a collection of shopkeepers who have in-depth knowledge about their local customers. He wants to make the company a place where customers are heard.

He also described Sears' desire to reach its customers at a grassroots level by adding the latest new technologies to the mix. According to Harles, "If you aren't really thinking about using social media in a grassroots way, it's merely window dressing."

He goes on to explain, "It's not good enough to just *listen* to the customer; [we need to] *do* something about it." Sears empowered its customers to say exactly what is on their minds by telling them that, "When you see something negative, you can truly resolve it."

Harles acknowledges that it's incredibly difficult for retailers in today's markets to differentiate themselves from one another. Whether it's pricing, products, or some other aspect, every retailer has to attract their target markets in one way or another. For Sears, it's service, the concept of providing value-based assistance for ordinary customers, by authentically being on their side and consistently available to serve them.

Sears monitors social chatter over the entire Web, and has base stations on Twitter, Facebook, and blogs. Twitter's @MySears voice belongs to the renowned Carla F., who seems to actually be able to be in more than one place at a time. With her cheery patter, she befriends her followers, solves problems, and tweets deals from the @SearsDeals account. There's also the @BlueToolCrew, @SearsHTS, and notices of crazy deals tweeted from @SearsOutlet.

Zappos

The first person to follow me on my original Twitter account was Tony Hsieh. Recall that I told you about his pioneering work at LinkExchange in Chapter 11; I'm mentioning him here because he's now the CEO of online shoe retailer Zappos.com.

My friend Tony has done more to bring business to social media than anyone else I can think of. Early on, he was the "official" tweeter on the Zappos account; he personally answered customer queries while chatting about his life and work. Tony was also one of the first corporate leaders to embrace this kind of customer service transparency.

From its inception, Zappos' raison d'être was to provide stellar customer service. Keeping its patrons happy was always the company's number one priority. Tony once famously said, "Our product is customer service. We are a service company that happens to be selling shoes."

Any customer who has an issue with any Zappos product can go to the customer service Frequently Asked Questions (FAQs) page at www.zappos.com/customer-service-center, where they'll find detailed instructions on how to solve almost any possible issue. And, since some people prefer to talk on the phone to a service representative, Zappos also has live people ready to take calls 24 hours a day, 365 days a year.

Offering free shipping (both ways, in case of a return—which Zappos covers by supplying prepaid return labels) and a one-year return policy, it's no wonder that Zappos.com customers have become the store's best evangelists. Tony turned an online retail site into a neighborhood of happy fans, who share their personal stories and photos with other community members.

This is all part of the company culture that Tony and his executive team have established throughout the organization. They firmly believe that all employees need to display the company spirit, and show that they truly support Zappos' core values. Their attitude is part of their annual reviews.

Staff members at every level of the company play a major role in its Twitter outreach. There are about 500 Zappos employees on Twitter, and their tweets are aggregated on the Zappos site at twitter.zappos.com/employee_tweets. Tony, himself, has a list of many on twitter.com/zappos/employees.

Zappos was purchased by Amazon.com last year for $1.2 billion, and it will be interesting to see whether the current, stellar company culture will survive and thrive.

By studying the styles of large companies, you as a small-business owner can better form your own online customer service persona. Every customer is different, as is every business. That is the reason customer service is considered a "soft science." You have to finesse your own style until you relate to your customers in the way that's best for you.

Index